Better Homes and Gardens®
fruit desserts
COOKING FOR TODAY

BETTER HOMES AND GARDENS® BOOKS
Des Moines

BETTER HOMES AND GARDENS® BOOKS
An Imprint of Meredith® Books

FRUIT DESSERTS
Editor: Mary Major Williams
Copy Chief: Gregory H. Kayko
Associate Art Director: Tom Wegner
Writer: DeAnne Hrabak
Copy Editor: Mary Helen Schiltz
Indexer: Kathleen Poole
Electronic Production Coordinator: Paula Forest
Test Kitchen Product Supervisors: Lynn Blanchard, Jennifer Peterson
Food Stylists: Lynn Blanchard, Janet Pittman, Jennifer Peterson
Photographers: Mike Dieter, Scott Little
Cover Photographer: Andy Lyons
Production Manager: Douglas Johnston

Director, New Product Development: Ray Wolf
Managing Editor: Christopher Cavanaugh
Test Kitchen Director: Sharon Stilwell

Meredith Publishing Group
President, Publishing Group: Christopher Little
Vice President and Publishing Director: John P. Loughlin

Meredith Corporation
Chairman of the Board and Chief Executive Officer: Jack D. Rehm
President and Chief Operating Officer: William T. Kerr

Chairman of the Executive Committee: E. T. Meredith III

On the cover: Honey-Fruit Pizza (see recipe, page 59)

All of us at Better Homes and Gardens® Books are dedicated to providing you with the information and ideas you need to create delicious foods. We welcome your comments and suggestions. Write to us at: Better Homes and Gardens® Books, Cookbook Editorial Department, RW-240, 1716 Locust St., Des Moines, IA 50309-3023

If you would like to order additional copies of any of our books, call 1-800-678-2803 or check with your local bookstore.

Our seal assures you that every recipe in *Fruit Desserts* has been tested in the Better Homes and Gardens® Test Kitchen. This means that each recipe is practical and reliable, and meets our high standards of taste appeal. We guarantee your satisfaction with this book for as long as you own it.

F resh fruit has long been sweetening our meals and making life more pleasurable. And now the health benefits make it an irresistible addition to any meal, anytime. Delicious by itself, fruit also serves as the springboard for memorable desserts too numerous to list.

This volume celebrates the wonderful desserts featuring fresh fruit. The variety is incredible. You'll find traditional favorites such as Old-Fashioned Apple Pie along with new dishes such as Tropical Fruit Plate with Berry Sauce. The health-conscious can spoon into light, refreshing Melon Sorbet, while the more indulgent can splurge on Double Raspberry Cheesecake. From the simple Fresh Berry Crisp to the festive Raspberry and Cream Torte, you'll find a dessert for every taste and every occasion on these pages. Take a look for yourself and enjoy.

CONTENTS

Every good cook knows that the juiciest pies, richest cobblers, and sweetest shortcakes begin with perfectly ripe, fresh fruit. On these pages you will learn how to select and handle top quality fruit for the most sumptuous desserts.

■ **Apples:** Apples are available fresh throughout the year. Choose firm apples with smooth unblemished skins without bruises or breaks. Brownish, freckled patches on the skin generally do not affect flavor. Apples purchased in a plastic bag can be stored that way in your refrigerator in the crisper drawer. Store apples purchased in bulk in a cool, moist place.

■ **Apricots:** Apricots are available from late May to mid-August. Look for plump, firm apricots with a red blush. Avoid fruit that is pale yellow or green-yellow, very firm, very soft, or bruised. Ripen firm fruit at room temperature until it yields to gentle pressure and is golden in color. Refrigerate ripe fruit up to 2 days.

■ **Bananas:** You can choose bananas in any stage of ripeness. Green bananas need to ripen several days before using. Bananas are ripe when they have a healthy yellow color with a few brown spots and, possibly, green tips. Use fully ripe bananas, which are soft and yellow but flecked with more brown, in recipes when mashed bananas are specified. Store bananas at room temperature until ripe. When bananas are the right color for your desired use, place them in the refrigerator until you need them. The peel turns black when the fruit is refrigerated, but the pulp stays at the desired ripeness for a few days.

■ **Berries:** Look for berries with healthy color for the particular variety. If picking your own, select berries that separate easily from their stems. Avoid bruised or moldy fruit. Refrigerate berries in a single layer, loosely covered. Heaping berries in a bowl or container will crush the delicate fruit. Use most berries within a day or two; however, blueberries will last from 10 to 14 days.

■ **Kiwi Fruit:** Kiwi fruit should yield to gentle pressure and have no bruises or soft spots. Ripen kiwi fruits at room temperature until they yield to gentle pressure, then refrigerate up to 1 week.

■ **Mangoes**: Mangoes are available from March through September. When ripe, mangoes should have a green to yellow skin tinged with red, smell fruity, and feel fairly firm when pressed gently. Avoid extremely soft or very bruised fruit or fruit with blemishes. Ripen mangoes at room temperature. Refrigerate them as soon as they are ripe and use them within 4 or 5 days.

■ **Melons:** All melons should feel heavy for their size and be well-shaped. Avoid fruit that is wet, dented, bruised, or cracked. Most melons, except watermelon, continue to ripen after picking. If a melon seems underripe, store it at room temperature for a few days. Then refrigerate it and use within 3 days.

■ **Nectarines:** Nectarines are at their peak between June and September. The red blush on nectarine skins is related to variety not ripeness. Look for fruit with a healthy golden yellow skin without tinges of green. Ripe nectarines should yield slightly to gentle pressure. Don't buy bruised or misshapen fruit. Nectarines are picked mature but firm for shipping. Complete the ripening at home by placing them in a loosely closed paper bag for several days at room temperature. Keep ripe nectarines in the refrigerator for 3 to 5 days.

■ **Papayas:** Choose papayas that are at least half yellow and feel somewhat soft when pressed. The skin should be smooth and free from bruises or soft spots. Ripen firm papayas at room temperature for 3 to 5 days until mostly yellow to yellowish-orange. Store ripe fruit in the refrigerator for up to 1 week.

■ **Peaches:** Choose fresh peaches that are firm to slightly soft when pressed. Skin color varies from golden yellow to dark reddish-brown, but the peaches should have no tinges of green. Look for well-shaped fruit without blemishes or soft spots. Ripen firm peaches at room temperature until they're slightly soft, then refrigerate the ripe fruit for up to 5 days.

■ **Pears:** Look for fresh pears without bruises or cuts. Skin color is not a good indicator of ripeness because the color of some varieties does not change as the fruit ripens. Place the firm pears in a paper bag or a loosely covered bowl. Let them stand at room temperature for a few days. Pears are ripe when they yield to gentle pressure at the stem end.

■ **Pineapple:** Look for a pineapple with a plump shape. Smell the stem end—it should be sweet and aromatic, not heavy or fermented. The pineapple should be slightly soft to the touch, heavy for its size, and have dark green leaves. Avoid those with mold, bruises, and dark, watery eyes. Refrigerate ripe pineapple for up to 2 days.

■ **Plums:** Look for firm, plump, well-shaped fresh plums with good color for the variety. Press a plum gently; it should give slightly. The light gray cast on the skin is natural protection and doesn't affect quality. Avoid overly soft, bruised, or exceptionally hard fruit. Ripen plums at room temperature, then refrigerate them for up to 5 days.

TROPICAL FRUIT PLATE WITH BERRY SAUCE

The strawberry-raspberry sauce is a cinch to make with the aid of a blender or food processor. Another time, ladle the sauce over ice cream, pound cake, or cheesecake.

½ cup fresh strawberries, rinsed and
     caps removed
½ cup fresh or frozen raspberries
2 tablespoons sugar
1 tablespoon lemon juice
2 ripe kiwi fruit
1 ripe mango or papaya
1 small fresh pineapple
1 orange
     Edible flowers, such as violets
        (optional)

For sauce, in a blender container or food processor bowl combine strawberries, raspberries, sugar, and lemon juice. Cover and blend or process till smooth. Strain through a fine sieve to remove seeds. Cover and chill sauce till serving time.

For kiwi fruit, using a small paring knife, remove the thin brown skin. Cut each kiwi fruit in half lengthwise; slice the halves.

For mango or papaya, use a sharp knife to remove peel; halve fruit. Cut mango flesh away from pit or spoon out seeds from papaya. Thinly slice the mango or papaya lengthwise.

For pineapple, twist off the crown (leaves). Using a sharp knife, cut off peel and remove eyes (brown spots). Slice fruit crosswise; cut slices in half and remove woody core.

For orange, slice the unpeeled orange crosswise. Cut each slice in half; remove any seeds.

Cover and chill all fruit till ready to serve. To serve, arrange fruit on dessert plates. Drizzle sauce over fruit. Garnish with flowers, if desired. Makes 4 servings.

Nutrition facts per serving: 158 calories, 1 g total fat (0 g saturated fat), 0 mg cholesterol, 4 mg sodium, 40 g carbohydrate, 5 g fiber, 2 g protein.
Daily Value: 21% vitamin A, 166% vitamin C, 3% calcium, 5% iron.

CHOCOLATE-DIPPED STRAWBERRIES

A truly memorable treat on their own, these yummy morsels also can decorate cakes, tortes, tarts, and many other festive desserts.

4 cups medium strawberries
6 ounces semisweet chocolate pieces
1 tablespoon shortening
6 ounces vanilla-flavored candy coating
1 cup finely chopped pecans or coconut
(optional)

Rinse strawberries. Gently pat dry with paper towels.

In a small glass mixing bowl combine semisweet chocolate pieces and shortening. Pour very warm tap water (100° to 110°) in a larger glass mixing bowl to a depth of 1 inch. Place small bowl containing chocolate inside larger bowl. Stir the chocolate mixture constantly with rubber spatula until the chocolate mixture is completely melted and smooth (about 20 minutes). Replace warm water as necessary, always removing bowl containing chocolate mixture before adding water to larger bowl. Do not allow any water to drip into chocolate.

Coarsely chop the vanilla-flavored candy coating. Place in a heavy small saucepan. Heat over low heat, stirring frequently till melted.

Dip *half* of the strawberries in the melted semisweet chocolate pieces, and the other half in the melted vanilla-flavored candy coating. To dip strawberries, hold each strawberry by the stem end and dip halfway into melted chocolate or candy coating. Allow excess chocolate or coating to drip off fruit. (Or, dip strawberry in both the melted candy coating and melted semisweet chocolate.) Place dipped berries on a baking sheet lined with waxed paper. If desired, immediately sprinkle chopped pecans or coconut onto dipped berries.

Let stand at least 1 hour at room temperature or till firm. Serve immediately or cover loosely with foil and chill in the refrigerator for 6 to 8 hours. Let chilled berries stand at room temperature about 30 minutes before serving. Makes about 30.

Nutrition facts per strawberry: 66 calories, 4 g total fat (1 g saturated fat), 0 mg cholesterol, 5 mg sodium, 9 g carbohydrate, 0 g fiber, 1 g protein.
Daily Value: 0% vitamin A, 18% vitamin C, 1% calcium, 1% iron.

POACHED PEARS WITH WHITE CHOCOLATE SAUCE

A rich, creamy white chocolate sauce drizzles down the sides of pears poached in sweet white wine for a company-pleasing dessert.

4 medium pears
1 cup sweet white wine
1 cup water
¼ cup sugar
1 teaspoon vanilla
   White Chocolate Sauce
   Fresh red raspberries (optional)

Peel pears, leaving stems intact. To core pears, use an apple corer or the rounded tip of a vegetable peeler. Push the corer or peeler through the blossom end of each pear, but do not cut through the stem end. Turn corer or peeler to loosen the core. Remove and discard core. Set pears aside.

In a large saucepan bring wine, water, sugar, and vanilla to boiling. Place the pears in the pan, stem ends up; spoon the wine mixture over the pears. Reduce heat. Cover and simmer for 15 to 20 minutes or till the pears are tender. Spoon some of the cooking liquid over the pears. Remove saucepan from heat. Let pears cool in liquid.

To serve, place each pear in a dessert dish. Spoon some of the cooking liquid over each. Drizzle with White Chocolate Sauce. Garnish with fresh raspberries, if desired. Makes 4 servings.

White Chocolate Sauce: In a small saucepan melt ¼ cup *white baking pieces* and 1 tablespoon *butter or margarine* over low heat. Add ⅓ cup *sugar*. Gradually stir in ½ cup *milk*. Bring to boiling; reduce heat. Boil gently over low heat for 8 minutes, stirring frequently. Remove from heat. Cool slightly (about 30 minutes).

Nutrition facts per serving: 311 calories, 7 g total fat (4 g saturated fat), 10 mg cholesterol, 57 mg sodium, 53 g carbohydrate., 5 g fiber, 2 g protein.
Daily Value: 4% vitamin A, 11% vitamin C, 7% calcium, 4% iron.

FRESH FRUIT WITH HONEY-LIME SAUCE

Sweet and juicy, fresh pineapple makes a wonderful addition to all kinds of fruit desserts. To simplify preparation, look for peeled and cored fresh pineapple in the produce section of your supermarket.

2 cups cut-up fresh pineapple
3 kiwi fruit, peeled, halved lengthwise, and sliced
1 medium papaya, peeled, seeded, and sliced
1 medium banana, sliced
¼ of a small watermelon, cut into wedges
2 tablespoons lime juice
   Honey-Lime Sauce

Arrange pineapple, kiwi fruit, papaya, banana, and watermelon on 6 dessert plates. Sprinkle with lime juice.

Spoon Honey-Lime Sauce over each serving. Serve immediately. Makes 6 servings.

Honey-Lime Sauce: In a medium mixing bowl stir together one 8-ounce container low-fat *vanilla yogurt,* 4 teaspoons *honey,* ½ teaspoon finely shredded *lime peel,* and 1 tablespoon *lime juice.*

Nutrition facts per serving: 144 calories, 1 g total fat (1 g saturated fat), 2 mg cholesterol, 26 mg sodium, 33 g carbohydrate, 3 g fiber, 3 g protein.
Daily Value: 8% vitamin A, 115% vitamin C, 6% calcium, 3% iron.

CHOCOLATE-GLAZED CARAMEL APPLES

Rolled in chopped peanuts and drizzled with chocolate, these scrumptious candied apples add a whimsical note to a dinner party.

6 large or 8 to 10 medium apples
20 ounces vanilla caramels (about 72)
3 tablespoons milk
2⅔ cups chopped peanuts
6 ounces semisweet chocolate,
    chocolate-flavored candy coating,
    or vanilla-flavored candy coating
1 tablespoon shortening

Wash and dry apples. Remove stems. Insert a wooden stick into the stem end of each apple. Set apples aside.

In a heavy medium saucepan combine unwrapped caramels and milk. Heat and stir over medium-low heat till caramels are melted. Remove from heat.

Dip each apple into the hot caramel mixture, spooning the caramel mixture evenly over the apple. Allow excess caramel mixture to drip off. (If the caramel mixture becomes too stiff, return to low heat and stir till soft again.) Immediately roll apples in chopped peanuts. Place apples, bottom sides down, on waxed paper. Let stand about 30 minutes or till firm.

Coarsely chop chocolate or candy coating. In a heavy medium saucepan combine chocolate or candy coating and shortening. Cook over low heat, stirring constantly, until the chocolate begins to melt. Remove saucepan from heat; stir till smooth. Spoon melted chocolate mixture over the caramel- and nut-coated apples, allowing chocolate to drip down the apple. Let stand till chocolate is firm.

To store, wrap apples in plastic wrap and place in a covered container. Store in the refrigerator for up to 1 week. Let stand at room temperature about 30 minutes before serving. Makes 6 servings.

Nutrition facts per serving: 1,044 calories, 53 g total fat (10 g saturated fat), 1 mg cholesterol, 256 mg sodium, 140 g carbohydrate, 12 g fiber, 22 g protein.
Daily Value: 2% vitamin A, 21% vitamin C, 19% calcium, 24% iron.

PINEAPPLE-ORANGE CREPES

If you like, make the crepes up to 2 days before serving them. Stack them with waxed paper between the layers and store in an airtight container in the refrigerator.

½ cup all-purpose flour
⅓ cup milk
1 egg
½ teaspoon finely shredded orange peel
⅓ cup orange juice
2 teaspoons cooking oil
½ of a fresh pineapple, peeled, cored, and sliced
2 tablespoons butter or margarine
¼ cup packed brown sugar
1 tablespoon cornstarch
½ cup orange juice
2 medium oranges, peeled and sectioned
1 tablespoon rum (optional)
¼ cup chopped pecans or toasted slivered almonds
¼ cup toasted coconut
   Fresh strawberries (optional)

For crepes, in a small mixing bowl combine flour, milk, egg, orange peel, ⅓ cup orange juice, and oil. Beat with a rotary beater till well mixed. Heat a lightly greased 6-inch skillet over medium heat. Spoon *2 tablespoons* of the batter into the skillet; lift and tilt the skillet to spread batter. Return to heat; brown on one side only. Invert pan over paper towels; remove crepe. Repeat with remaining batter, greasing skillet occasionally.

Fold each crepe in half, browned side out. Fold in half again forming a triangle. Place in a single layer on a baking sheet. Keep crepes warm in a 300° oven while making sauce.

For sauce, cut the pineapple slices into fourths; set aside. In a medium saucepan melt butter or margarine. Stir in brown sugar and cornstarch. Add ½ cup orange juice. Cook and stir till thickened and bubbly. Cook and stir for 1 minute more. Add pineapple, orange sections, and, if desired, rum. Cook over low heat, stirring gently, till heated through.

Arrange folded crepes on dessert plates. Spoon sauce over crepes. Sprinkle with nuts and coconut. Garnish with fresh strawberries, if desired. Makes 4 servings.

Nutrition facts per serving: 345 calories, 17 g total fat (5 g saturated fat), 70 mg cholesterol, 102 mg sodium, 45 g carbohydrate, 3 g fiber, 6 g protein.
***Daily Value:** 10% vitamin A, 85% vitamin C, 5% calcium, 11% iron.*

BEST-EVER BAKED APPLES

Always a favorite, this versatile recipe for baked apples offers 5 equally delicious fillings. Try a different one every time. The apple in the photograph is filled with the Dried Fruit Filling.

4 large baking apples
    (about 1¾ pounds)
    Desired Filling (see fillings, right)
⅓ cup apple juice, cider, or dry
    white wine
    Sweetened whipped cream, vanilla
    yogurt, light cream, or frozen
    vanilla yogurt (optional)
    Ground nutmeg (optional)

To core apples, use an apple corer or the rounded tip of a vegetable peeler. Push corer or peeler most of the way through the apple center, but do not cut through the other end; turn corer or peeler to loosen the upper part of the core. Remove and discard core. Enlarge hole slightly at top of the apple for filling.

Remove the peel from the top half of each apple. Place apples in a 2-quart square baking dish. Spoon desired filling into center of each apple. Add juice, cider, or wine to the dish. Cover with foil.

Bake in a 350° oven about 45 minutes or till apples are fork-tender. Transfer apples to dessert dishes; spoon liquid in dish over apples. Serve warm. If desired, serve with whipped cream, yogurt, light cream, or frozen yogurt and sprinkle with nutmeg. Makes 4 servings.

Dried Fruit: Mix ⅔ cup *raisins, currants, or mixed dried fruit bits;* 2 tablespoons *brown sugar;* and ½ teaspoon ground *cinnamon.*

Ginger-Almond: Mix 1 tablespoon chopped *crystallized ginger,* ¼ cup slivered *almonds or pine nuts,* and 2 tablespoons *apricot preserves.*

Orange-Macaroon: Toss together ⅔ cup crumbled *soft coconut macaroon cookies* and 2 tablespoons *orange marmalade.*

Peanut Butter: Mix ⅓ cup *coconut* and ⅓ cup *chunky peanut butter.*

Apple-Walnut: Mix ⅓ cup *apple butter* and ¼ cup chopped *walnuts.*

Nutrition facts per serving with dried fruit filling: 225 calories, 1 g total fat (0 g saturated fat), 0 mg cholesterol, 7 mg sodium, 59 g carbohydrate, 6 g fiber, 1 g protein. **Daily Value:** *1% vitamin A, 21% vitamin C, 3% calcium, 7% iron.*

FRUIT AND CREAM WITH DIAMOND SNAPS

Crisp almond-scented cookies pair delightfully with this fresh fruit combo.

¼ cup packed brown sugar
3 tablespoons cooking oil
2 tablespoons light corn syrup
1 teaspoon lemon juice
1 teaspoon water
¼ teaspoon almond extract
⅓ cup all-purpose flour
6 cups fresh fruit, such as cut-up, peeled
   kiwi fruit, bananas, or pears;
   quartered strawberries; blueberries
   or seedless red or green grapes
Yogurt Cream

For diamond snaps, in a medium mixing bowl combine brown sugar, oil, corn syrup, lemon juice, water, and almond extract. Add flour; stir till combined. Line a 15x10x1-inch baking pan with foil; grease foil generously. Spread batter over foil in a 10x6-inch rectangle. Bake in a 350° oven for 13 to 14 minutes or till mixture is bubbly and deep golden brown. (The mixture will spread during baking.)

Transfer pan to a wire rack; cool for 2 minutes or till slightly set. Score cookies into 2-inch diamonds; let cool for 1 minute more. Remove from foil; break into diamonds.

Arrange fruit on 8 dessert plates. Serve with diamond snaps and Yogurt Cream. Makes 8 servings.

Yogurt Cream: In a small mixing bowl combine one 8-ounce carton *vanilla yogurt* and one 8-ounce container *fruit-flavored soft-style cream cheese.* Beat with an electric mixer on low speed till combined.

Nutrition facts per serving: 282 calories, 14 g total fat (6 g saturated fat), 26 mg cholesterol, 114 mg sodium, 38 g carbohydrate, 3 g fiber, 3 g protein.
Daily Value: 6% vitamin A, 60% vitamin C, 6% calcium, 6% iron.

GINGERED MELON

Enjoy this cool, refreshing melon cup on the hottest days of summer.

¾ cup water
½ cup sugar
2 teaspoons finely shredded lemon peel
    (set aside)
4 teaspoons lemon juice
1½ to 2 teaspoons grated fresh gingerroot
4 cups watermelon, cantaloupe, and/or
    honeydew balls
⅓ cup flaked coconut

For syrup, in a small saucepan combine water, sugar, lemon juice, and gingerroot. Cook over medium heat till boiling. Reduce heat and simmer, uncovered, for 3 minutes. Remove from heat; stir in lemon peel. Cool to room temperature. Strain, if desired.

Pour syrup over melon balls. Stir gently to coat. Cover and chill for 2 to 24 hours. To serve, spoon melon balls and syrup into 6 dessert dishes. Sprinkle with coconut. Makes 6 servings.

Nutrition facts per serving: 122 calories, 2 g total fat (1 g saturated fat), 0 mg cholesterol, 10 mg sodium, 28 g carbohydrate, 1 g fiber, 1 g protein.
Daily Value: 13% vitamin A, 53% vitamin C, 0% calcium, 1% iron.

APPLES WITH CINNAMON-CIDER DIP

Once cut, the apple slices brown quickly. Sprinkle them with lemon or orange juice mixed with a little water, or treat them with an ascorbic acid color keeper.

2   tablespoons cornstarch
1   tablespoon brown sugar
1¼ cups apple cider
3   tablespoons honey
2   teaspoons lemon juice
½   teaspoon ground cinnamon
⅛   teaspoon salt (optional)
    Dash cloves
    Dash allspice
1   tablespoon butter or margarine
4   apples, cored and sliced

For dip, in a medium saucepan combine cornstarch and brown sugar. Stir in apple cider, honey, lemon juice, cinnamon, salt (if desired), cloves, and allspice. Cook and stir till thickened and bubbly. Cook and stir for 2 minutes more. Remove from heat. Add butter or margarine; stir till melted.

Serve dip warm with sliced apples. Makes 4 to 6 servings.

Nutrition facts per servings: 221 calories, 3 g total fat, (2 g saturated fat), 8 mg cholesterol, 34 mg sodium, 51 g carbohydrate, 3 g fiber, 0 g protein.
Daily Value: 3% vitamin A, 16% vitamin C, 1% calcium,) 6% iron.

SPIKED FRUIT IN PINEAPPLE BOATS

Although we filled these pineapple shells with a mixture of pineapple, mango, berries, and kiwi fruit, use 5½ cups of any cut-up fresh fruit you wish.

1 medium pineapple
1 medium mango or papaya
1 cup blueberries and/or halved
    strawberries
2 kiwi fruit, peeled, quartered,
    and sliced
½ cup berry-flavored wine cooler
2 tablespoons powdered sugar
¼ teaspoon ground nutmeg

Cut the pineapple lengthwise into quarters. Use a thin paring knife or grapefruit knife to remove the fruit of the pineapple from each quarter, leaving a shell ¼ to ½ inch thick. Set shells aside. Remove the core from the pineapple pieces. Cut into bite-size pieces; set aside.

To prepare the mango, cut lengthwise through the mango, sliding a sharp knife next to the seed along one side of the mango. Repeat on other side of the seed. Cut away all of the fruit that remains around the seed. Remove the peel. Cut the fruit into bite-size pieces. (To prepare the papaya, cut lengthwise in half and scoop out seeds. Peel and cut into bite-size pieces.)

In a large mixing bowl combine the cut-up pineapple, mango or papaya, blueberries and/or strawberries, and kiwi fruit. Pour wine cooler over fruit. Sprinkle with powdered sugar and nutmeg. Toss gently to mix. To serve, spoon fruit mixture into pineapple shells. Makes 4 servings.

Nutrition facts per serving: 181 calories, 1 g total fat (0 g saturated fat), 0 mg cholesterol, 9 mg sodium, 44 g carbohydrate., 5 g fiber, 2 g protein.
Daily Value: 21% vitamin A, 134% vitamin C, 2% calcium, 6% iron.

Spiked Fruit in Melon Boats: Prepare as directed above except substitute 1 medium *cantaloupe* for the pineapple. Cut the cantaloupe lengthwise into quarters. Remove the seeds. Using a grapefruit knife or another knife cut the fruit from each quarter leaving a shell ¼ to ½ inch thick. Set shells aside. Cut the fruit into bite-size pieces.

Nutrition facts per serving: 161 calories, 1 g total fat (0 g saturated fat), 0 mg cholesterol, 22 mg sodium, 38 g carbohydrate., 5 g fiber, 2 g protein.
Daily Value: 72% vitamin A, 207% vitamin C, 3% calcium, 4% iron.

FRESH FRUIT WITH MOCHA FONDUE

Dessert fondues encourage lingering over the dinner table with good conversation. For a truly memorable dessert, we added coffee crystals and coffee liqueur to a rich chocolate fondue.

1 4-ounce package sweet baking chocolate, broken up
4 ounces semisweet chocolate, chopped
⅔ cup half-and-half, light cream, or milk
½ cup sifted powdered sugar
1 teaspoon instant coffee crystals
2 tablespoons coffee liqueur
   Assorted fresh fruit (such as apricot wedges, pear wedges, plum wedges, strawberries, pineapple chunks, kiwi fruit wedges, banana slices)

In a heavy medium saucepan combine sweet baking chocolate; semisweet chocolate; half-and-half, light cream, or milk; powdered sugar; and coffee crystals. Heat and stir over low heat till melted and smooth. Remove from heat; stir in liqueur.

Pour into a fondue pot; keep warm over low heat. Serve with fresh fruit as dippers. Makes 6 to 8 servings.

Nutrition facts per serving: 305 calories, 16 g total fat (10 g saturated fat), 10 mg cholesterol, 13 mg sodium, 43 g carbohydrate, 2 g fiber, 3 g protein. Daily Value: 3% vitamin A, 0% vitamin C, 3% calcium, 7% iron.

RED AND GREEN GRAPES WITH CRÈME FRÂICHE

Crème Frâiche (krem FRESH) is often used with fresh fruit in French cooking. Its tangy flavor blends delightfully with sweet grapes in this easy dessert.

Crème Frâiche
3 tablespoons brown sugar
½ teaspoon vanilla
2 cups seedless red grapes
1 cup seedless green grapes

In a large mixing bowl stir together Crème Frâiche, brown sugar, and vanilla; set aside.

Toss together red and green grapes. Spoon grapes into dessert dishes. Drizzle with Crème Frâiche mixture. Makes 6 servings.

Crème Frâiche: In a small mixing bowl stir together ¼ cup *whipping cream* (not ultrapasteurized) and ¼ cup *dairy sour cream.* Cover with plastic wrap. Let stand at room temperature for 2 to 5 hours or till mixture thickens. When thickened, cover and chill in the refrigerator till serving time. Stir before serving.

Nutrition facts per serving: 134 calories, 6 g total fat (4 g saturated fat), 18 mg cholesterol, 12 mg sodium, 20 g carbohydrate, 1 g fiber, 1 g protein.
Daily Value: 7% vitamin A, 14% vitamin C, 2% calcium, 2% iron.

MAPLE-GLAZED BANANAS

Warm and buttery, the maple sauce flavors every scrumptious bite of this rich dessert.

½   cup butter or margarine
½   cup packed brown sugar
½   cup maple or maple-flavored syrup
1   teaspoon finely shredded lemon peel
1   tablespoon lemon juice
¼   teaspoon ground cloves
6   firm, ripe bananas, halved lengthwise
     and cut into 1-inch pieces
1   quart vanilla ice cream

In large heavy skillet melt butter or margarine over medium heat. Stir in brown sugar, syrup, lemon peel, lemon juice, and cloves. Bring to boiling. Reduce heat; simmer for 2 minutes. Add bananas; spoon some of the syrup mixture over bananas. Cover and cook about 2 minutes more or till heated through. Remove from heat.

Scoop ice cream into dessert dishes. Spoon warm bananas and syrup over ice cream. Makes 8 servings.

Nutrition facts per serving: 403 calories, 19 g total fat (12 g saturated fat), 60 mg cholesterol, 175 mg sodium, 60 g carbohydrate, 2 g fiber, 3 g protein.
Daily Value: 18% vitamin A, 15% vitamin C, 8% calcium, 5% iron.

BERRY AND SOUR CREAM PIE

Tangy sour cream and juicy sweet berries merge for a perfect partnership in this luscious pie.

1 cup graham cracker crumbs
¼ cup finely chopped pecans or walnuts
2 tablespoons all-purpose flour
1 tablespoon sugar
⅓ cup butter or margarine, melted
½ cup sugar
3 tablespoons cornstarch
1 teaspoon unflavored gelatin
1⅓ cups milk
1½ cups dairy sour cream
1 tablespoon vanilla
3 cups red raspberries, blueberries, and/or sliced strawberries
1 strawberry, sliced (optional)

For crust, in a small mixing bowl combine graham cracker crumbs, pecans or walnuts, flour, and the 1 tablespoon sugar. Stir in melted butter or margarine. Toss to mix well. Press mixture onto the bottom and up sides of a 9-inch pie plate. Bake in a 375° oven for 8 minutes. Cool on a wire rack.

For filling, in a medium saucepan combine the ½ cup sugar, cornstarch, and gelatin; stir in milk. Cook and stir over medium heat till thickened and bubbly; cook and stir for 2 minutes more. Place sour cream in a medium mixing bowl. Gradually stir hot milk mixture into the sour cream; stir in vanilla. Cover with plastic wrap and chill in the refrigerator for 1 hour, stirring once or twice.

Stir berries into the sour cream mixture. Turn filling into the cooled crust. Cover and chill at least 6 hours or up to 24 hours. Garnish with sliced strawberry, if desired. Makes 8 servings.

Nutrition facts per serving: 352 calories, 21 g total fat (11 g saturated fat), 43 mg cholesterol, 181 mg sodium, 38 g carbohydrate, 2 g fiber, 5 g protein.
***Daily Value:** 20% vitamin A, 29% vitamin C, 9% calcium, 5% iron.*

APPLE-MINCEMEAT DUMPLINGS

For this old-fashioned dessert, apples are stuffed with mincemeat and chopped nuts, wrapped in flaky pastry, and baked in a brown sugar sauce.

½ cup prepared mincemeat
3 tablespoons chopped pecans
2 tablespoons orange marmalade
1 tablespoon butter or margarine, melted
    Pastry for Double-Crust Pie (see recipe, page 44)
6 medium baking apples, peeled and cored
2 cups packed brown sugar
1¼ cups water
2 tablespoons lemon juice or orange juice
½ teaspoon ground cinnamon
¼ teaspoon salt

Grease a 13x9x2-inch baking pan. In a small mixing bowl stir together mincemeat, pecans, marmalade, and butter or margarine. Set aside.

Roll out pastry to an 18x12-inch rectangle. Cut into six 6-inch squares. Place an apple in the center of each pastry square. Fill center cavities with the mincemeat mixture. Moisten corners of each pastry square and bring corners up over apple, pinching to seal. Pinch remaining edges of pastry to seal. Place dumplings in prepared pan. Bake in a 375° oven for 30 minutes.

Meanwhile, for sauce, in a medium saucepan stir together brown sugar, water, lemon juice or orange juice, cinnamon, and salt. Heat to boiling. Spoon about *half* of the sauce over dumplings. Bake for 15 to 20 minutes more, basting dumplings with sauce several times.

With a metal spatula carefully loosen dumplings from pan. Serve warm with remaining syrup. Makes 6 servings.

Nutrition facts per serving: 752 calories, 28 g total fat (7 g saturated fat), 5 mg cholesterol, 289 mg sodium, 126 g carbohydrate, 5 g fiber, 5 g protein.
Daily Value: 2% vitamin A, 11% vitamin C, 6% calcium, 26% iron.

KIWI-LIME PIE

This delightful pie features 2 pastry layers sandwiched between a creamy lime filling.

¾   cup sugar
⅓   cup all-purpose flour
⅛   teaspoon salt
1¾ cups milk
3   beaten eggs
¼   cup butter or margarine
2   teaspoons finely shredded lime peel
¼   cup lime juice
1   8-ounce carton lemon yogurt
    Few drops green food coloring
    Pastry for Double-Crust Pie
       (see recipe, page 44)
¼   cup apple jelly
    Sweetened Whipped Cream
       (see recipe, page 116) (optional)
2   kiwi fruits, peeled, halved lengthwise,
       and sliced (optional)
1   or 2 lime slices (optional)

For filling, in a medium saucepan combine sugar, flour, and salt. Stir in milk. Cook and stir over medium heat till thickened and bubbly. Reduce heat; cook and stir for 2 minutes more. Remove from heat. Stir *1 cup* of the hot mixture into eggs. Return to saucepan; cook and stir till thickened. Cook and stir for 2 minutes more. *Do not boil.* Remove from heat. Stir in butter or margarine, lime peel, and juice. Fold in yogurt. Tint with food coloring. Cover surface of filling with plastic wrap; cool.

On a floured surface roll *half* of the pastry into a 12-inch circle. Line a 9-inch pie plate with pastry. Trim and flute edge; prick pastry. Bake in a 450° oven for 10 to 12 minutes. Cool.

Divide remaining pastry in half. Roll each half into circles ⅛ inch thick; cut an 8¾-inch circle out of one portion and an 8-inch circle out of other portion. Place circles on a baking sheet; prick pastry. Bake in 450° oven for 10 minutes. Cool.

Brush the pastry shell with some of the jelly. Place about *1 cup* of the filling in pastry shell. Cover with 8-inch pastry round; brush with jelly. Spread with 1¼ *cups* of filling. Top with the 8¾-inch pastry. Brush with remaining jelly. Top with remaining custard. Cover; chill pie overnight. If desired, garnish with Sweetened Whipped Cream, kiwi fruit slices, and lime slices just before serving. Makes 8 servings.

Nutrition facts per serving: 507 calories, 26 g total fat (9 g saturated fat), 100 mg cholesterol, 294 mg sodium, 60 g carbohydrate, 1 g fiber, 9 g protein.
Daily Value: 12% vitamin A, 6% vitamin C, 10% calcium, 13% iron.

APPLE TURNOVERS

Enjoy these flaky pastries with a glass of ice cold milk.

1   17¼-ounce package (2 sheets) frozen
       puff pastry
⅓   cup sugar
4   teaspoons all-purpose flour
1   teaspoon finely shredded lemon peel
½   teaspoon ground allspice or cinnamon
3   medium cooking apples, peeled,
       cored and coarsely chopped
       (about 3 cups)
⅓   cup raisins (optional)
1   tablespoon milk
2   tablespoons sugar

Let folded pastry thaw at room temperature for 20 minutes. On a lightly floured surface, unfold 1 sheet of pastry and roll into an 11-inch square. Cut pastry into four 5½-inch squares. Repeat with remaining pastry. You will have a total of 8 pastry squares.

In a medium mixing bowl stir together ⅓ cup sugar, flour, lemon peel, and allspice or cinnamon. Add apples and, if desired, raisins. Toss to coat. Spoon about *⅓ cup* of the filling onto each pastry square. Moisten edges of pastry with a little water. Fold each pastry square in half diagonally, sealing edges well by pressing with a fork.

Place on ungreased baking sheet. Brush lightly with milk. Sprinkle with the 2 tablespoons sugar. Cut 2 or 3 slits in the top of each pastry to allow steam to escape. Bake in a 375° oven about 30 minutes or till golden. Transfer turnovers to wire rack. Serve warm or cool. Makes 8 servings.

Nutrition facts per serving: 342 calories, 19 g total fat (0 g saturated fat), 0 mg cholesterol, 231 mg sodium, 41 g carbohydrate., 1 g fiber, 3 g protein.
***Daily Value:** 0% vitamin A, 3% vitamin C, 0% calcium, 0% iron*

PLUM DUMPLINGS

To make 8 of these plump dumplings, use Pastry for Double-Crust Pie (see recipe, page 44) and double the remaining ingredients.

Pastry for Single-Crust Pie
    (see recipe, page 50)
3 tablespoons brown sugar
2 teaspoons butter or margarine
⅛ teaspoon ground cloves
    Dash ground nutmeg
4 ripe purple plums
1 tablespoon milk
4 teaspoons granulated sugar
¼ teaspoon ground cinnamon
    Vanilla or cinnamon ice cream
      (optional)

Prepare pastry. On a lightly floured surface, roll pastry into an 11-inch circle. Cut into four 5½-inch squares. If desired, cut small leaf shapes from any remaining pastry.

In a small mixing bowl stir together brown sugar, butter or margarine, cloves, and nutmeg; set aside.

For each dumpling, cut 1 plum in half and remove pit. Spoon *one-fourth* of the brown sugar mixture onto 1 plum half; replace remaining half. Place the filled plum on a pastry square. Bring up corners of dough and pinch edges and corners together to seal. Place dumpling in a shallow baking pan. Brush with milk. Decorate dumplings with pastry leaves, pressing firmly to secure. Stir together granulated sugar and cinnamon; sprinkle over dumplings.

Bake in a 375° oven about 35 minutes or till pastry is brown. Serve warm and, if desired, with ice cream. Makes 4 servings.

Nutrition facts per serving: 385 calories, 20 g total fat (6 g saturated fat), 5 mg cholesterol, 158 mg sodium, 49 g carbohydrate, 2 g fiber, 4 g protein.
Daily Value: 4% vitamin A, 10% vitamin C, 1% calcium, 13% iron.

OLD-FASHIONED APPLE PIE

Our version of the quintessential American dessert is bursting with apples and perfectly spiced.

6   cups peeled, thinly sliced tart apples
1   tablespoon lemon juice
½   cup granulated sugar
¼   cup all-purpose flour
¼   cup packed brown sugar
½   teaspoon ground cinnamon
¼   teaspoon ground nutmeg
    Dash ground cloves
    Pastry for Double-Crust Pie
1   tablespoon butter or margarine
    Milk (optional)
    Shredded cheddar cheese (optional)

In a large mixing bowl toss apples with lemon juice. Combine granulated sugar, flour, brown sugar, cinnamon, nutmeg, and cloves. Toss till apples are coated. Set apple mixture aside.

Prepare Pastry for Double-Crust Pie. Divide dough in half. Form each half into a ball. On a lightly floured surface, roll out 1 ball of dough into a 12-inch circle. Ease pastry into a 9-inch pie plate.

Transfer apple mixture to pastry-lined pie plate. Dot with butter or margarine. Trim pastry even with pie plate. For top crust, roll out remaining dough. Cut slits in top crust. Place top crust on the filling. Seal and flute the edge. Brush with milk, if desired.

To prevent overbrowning, cover the edge of the pie with foil. Bake in a 375° oven for 25 minutes. Remove foil; bake for 20 to 25 minutes more or till the top is golden brown and apples are tender. Serve warm with cheddar cheese, if desired. Makes 6 to 8 servings.

Pastry for Double-Crust Pie: Stir together 2 cups *all-purpose flour* and 1 teaspoon *salt.* Cut in ⅔ cup *shortening.* Sprinkle 6 to 7 tablespoons *cold water,* 1 tablespoon at a time, over the flour mixture, tossing gently after each addition till all is moistened. Form dough into a ball.

Nutrition facts per serving: 534 calories, 26 g total fat (7 g saturated fat), 5 mg cholesterol, 201 mg sodium, 74 g carbohydrate, 4 g fiber, 5 g protein.
Daily Value: 2% vitamin A, 12% vitamin C, 2% calcium, 16% iron.

BERRIES IN A CLOUD

Between the feather-light meringue and the juicy red berries, you'll find a layer of sinfully delicious chocolate-cream cheese mousse.

3   egg whites
1   teaspoon vanilla
¼   teaspoon cream of tartar
1   cup granulated sugar
½   cup finely chopped almonds, toasted
1   3-ounce package cream cheese, softened
½   cup packed brown sugar
½   cup unsweetened cocoa powder
2   tablespoons milk
½   teaspoon vanilla
1   cup whipping cream
3   cups fresh whole strawberries, stems and caps removed
2   ounces semisweet chocolate, cut up
2   teaspoons shortening

Let egg whites stand at room temperature for 30 minutes. Cover a baking sheet with plain brown paper or parchment paper. Draw a 9-inch circle on the paper; set aside.

In a large mixing bowl combine egg whites, 1 teaspoon vanilla, and cream of tartar. Beat with electric mixer on medium speed till soft peaks form. Gradually add granulated sugar, *1 tablespoon* at a time, beating on high speed till very stiff peaks form (tips stand straight) and sugar is almost dissolved. Fold in almonds. Spread over circle drawn on paper, building sides up taller than center to form a shell.

Bake in a 300° oven for 45 minutes. Turn off oven; let meringue dry in oven with door closed at least 1 hour (*do not* open oven door). Remove from oven. Lift meringue and carefully peel off paper; transfer to a serving platter. (Or, store in an airtight container overnight.)

For cocoa mousse, in a small mixing bowl beat cream cheese and brown sugar till smooth. Add cocoa powder, milk, and the ½ teaspoon vanilla; beat till smooth. In another chilled, small mixing bowl beat whipping cream with chilled beaters of an electric mixer on medium speed to soft peaks; fold into cocoa mixture.

Carefully spoon cocoa mousse into the meringue shell. Press whole berries, stem side down, into the mousse. In a heavy small saucepan melt semisweet chocolate and shortening over low heat, stirring constantly. Drizzle over berries, filling, and meringue. Serve immediately, or cover and chill filled meringue for up to 2 hours. To serve, cut into wedges, dipping knife in water between cuts. Makes 10 servings.

Nutrition facts per serving: 327 calories, 18 g total fat (9 g saturated fat), 42 mg cholesterol, 56 mg sodium, 40 g carbohydrate, 2 g fiber, 5 g protein.
Daily Value: 14% vitamin A, 42% vitamin C, 9% calcium, 10% iron.

APPLE-BLUEBERRY PASTRIES

Take a platter of these petite pastries to your next potluck.

2 tablespoons sugar
1 tablespoon cornstarch
2 medium apples, cored, peeled, and
   chopped (about 2 cups)
½ cup fresh or frozen blueberries
1½ teaspoons water
½ teaspoon finely shredded orange peel
1 17¼-ounce package (2 sheets) frozen
   puff pastry
   Water
   Easy Orange Icing
   Edible flowers (optional)

Line a large baking sheet with foil; set aside.

For filling, in a medium saucepan stir together sugar and cornstarch. Add apples, blueberries, and 1½ teaspoons water. Cook and stir over medium heat till thickened and bubbly. Cook and stir for 2 minutes more. Stir in orange peel. Remove from heat. Cool completely.

Let folded puff pastry thaw at room temperature for 20 minutes.

On a lightly floured surface, unfold 1 sheet of pastry and roll into a 15x10-inch rectangle. Cut ten 5x3-inch rectangles. Repeat with remaining pastry. You will have a total of 20 pastry rectangles.

Spoon about *1 tablespoon* of the filling on half of each small rectangle to within ½ inch of each end. Brush the edge of the pastry with water. Starting from one of the short sides, lift dough up and over filling. Press edges with the tines of a fork to seal. Place pastry on foil-lined baking sheet.

Bake in a 375° oven for 18 to 20 minutes or till golden. Remove from baking sheet. Cool on a wire rack. Drizzle with Easy Orange Icing. Arrange pastries on a dessert platter; garnish with edible flowers, if desired. Makes 20.

Easy Orange Icing: In a small mixing bowl stir together 1 cup sifted *powdered sugar,* 1 tablespoon *orange juice,* and ¼ teaspoon *vanilla.* Stir in additional orange juice, 1 teaspoon at a time, till the icing is of drizzling consistency.

Nutrition facts per pastry: 142 calories, 8 g total fat (0 g saturated fat), 0 mg cholesterol, 92 mg sodium, 18 g carbohydrate., 0 g fiber, 1 g protein.
Daily Value: 0% vitamin A, 2% vitamin C, 0% calcium, 0% iron.

CONCORD GRAPE PIE

Best known for jam and grape juice, Concord grapes make a wonderful pie as well. Look for fresh Concord grapes in September and October in grocery stores and at farmer's markets.

Pastry for Single-Crust Pie
1½   pounds Concord grapes (4 cups)
¾   cup sugar
⅓   cup all-purpose flour
¼   teaspoon salt
2   tablespoons butter or margarine, melted
1   tablespoon lemon juice
⅔   cup all-purpose flour
⅔   cup sugar
⅓   cup butter or margarine

Prepare Pastry for Single-Crust Pie; set aside.

Remove skins from grapes by gently pressing each grape between your fingers. The skins will slip off easily. Set skins aside. In a large saucepan bring grape pulp to boiling. Reduce heat and simmer, uncovered, for 5 minutes. Sieve the pulp to remove the seeds. Add the grape skins to the pulp.

In a large mixing bowl stir together the ¾ cup sugar, the ⅓ cup flour, and salt. Stir in the grape mixture, the 2 tablespoons melted butter or margarine, and the lemon juice. Pour into the pastry-lined pie plate. To prevent overbrowning, cover the edge of the pie with foil. Bake in a 375° oven for 20 minutes.

Meanwhile, stir together the ⅔ cup flour and the ⅔ cup sugar. Cut in the ⅓ cup butter or margarine till mixture resembles coarse crumbs. Remove foil from pie. Sprinkle crumb mixture over pie. Bake about 25 minutes more or till topping is golden. Cool on a wire rack. Makes 8 servings.

Pastry for Single-Crust Pie: In a medium mixing bowl stir together 1¼ cups *all-purpose flour* and ¼ teaspoon *salt*. Cut in ⅓ cup *shortening* till pieces are the size of small peas. Sprinkle 3 to 4 tablespoons *cold water*, 1 tablespoon at a time, over mixture, tossing gently till all is moistened. Form dough into a ball. On a lightly floured surface, roll dough into a 12-inch circle. Fit into a 9-inch pie plate. Trim to ½ inch beyond edge; fold under pastry and flute edge.

Nutrition facts per serving: 410 calories, 18 g total fat (8 g saturated fat), 23 mg cholesterol, 222 mg sodium, 62 g carbohydrate, 2 g fiber, 3 g protein.
***Daily value:** 8% vitamin A, 4% vitamin C, 1% calcium, 10% iron.*

CHERRY-PEAR TARTS

These individual double-crust pies make generous servings that will satisfy the heartiest of appetites.

2¾ cups sliced, peeled pears or apples
1   cup fresh or frozen pitted tart red
    cherries
½   cup sugar
1   tablespoon all-purpose flour
1   tablespoon cherry or apple brandy
    or apple juice
⅛   teaspoon ground nutmeg
    Pastry for Double-Crust Pie
    (see recipe, page 44)
2   teaspoons milk
2   teaspoons sugar

For filling, in a large mixing bowl combine pears or apples, cherries, the ½ cup sugar, flour, brandy or apple juice, and nutmeg; toss to mix. (If using frozen cherries, let stand for 15 to 30 minutes or till cherries are partially thawed.)

Prepare pastry. On a lightly floured surface, roll out *half* of the dough to ⅛-inch thickness. Cut pastry into four 6½-inch circles. Line four 4½-inch individual pie plates or tart pans with pastry. Trim to ¼ inch beyond edge of the tart pans.

Fill pastry-lined pie plates with filling. For top crusts, roll out and cut remaining pastry as directed above. Cut slits in top crusts. Adjust top crusts. Seal and flute edges. Brush tops of tarts with milk. Sprinkle with the 2 teaspoons sugar. Cover edges of tarts with foil. Place tarts on a baking sheet.

Bake in a 375° oven for 20 minutes (30 minutes if using frozen fruit). Remove foil. Bake for 10 to 15 minutes more or till pastry is golden and filling is bubbly. Cool on a wire rack. Makes 4 servings.

Nutrition facts per serving: 726 calories, 35 g total fat (9 g saturated fat), 0 mg cholesterol, 271 mg sodium, 96 g carbohydrate, 6 g fiber, 7 g protein.
Daily Value: 5% vitamin A, 14% vitamin C, 2% calcium, 21% iron.

POACHED FRUIT TART

Delicately spiced summer fruits nestle in a hazelnut cookie crust for an eye-catching, as well as tasty, dessert.

3   cups sweet white wine
       (such as Reisling)
2   cups sugar
4   inches stick cinnamon
4   whole cloves
4   apricots, halved and pitted
4   plums, quartered and pitted
8   fresh figs, halved or quartered
       Cinnamon-Hazelnut Tart Crust

In a large saucepan combine wine, sugar, cinnamon, and cloves. Bring to simmering. Cook apricots in the syrup for 3 minutes or till almost tender. Remove with a slotted spoon; drain. Repeat with plums, cooking about 3 minutes, and figs, cooking about 4 minutes. Peel apricots; set aside.

Remove the cinnamon and cloves from syrup. Measure ⅔ cup of syrup and transfer to a small saucepan. Boil gently about 10 minutes or till reduced by half; remove from heat.

Arrange the poached fruits in Cinnamon-Hazelnut Tart Crust; brush with reduced syrup. Serve immediately. Makes 12 servings.

Cinnamon-Hazelnut Tart Crust: In a large mixing bowl combine 2 cups *all-purpose flour,* ½ cup coarsely ground toasted *hazelnuts,* 2 tablespoons *sugar,* 1 teaspoon ground *cinnamon,* and a dash *salt.* Cut in ¾ cup cold *butter or margarine* till crumbly. Add ⅓ cup *ice water.* Knead quickly till mixture forms a ball. Roll out into a ¼-inch-thick round. Line a fluted, 11-inch tart pan with the dough, pressing it into the fluted edges. Trim edges even with rim of pan. Prick generously with a fork. Bake in a 400° oven for 15 minutes. Cool on a wire rack.

Nutrition facts per serving: 295 calories, 15 g fat (7 g saturated fat), 31 mg cholesterol, 129 mg sodium, 37 g carbohydrate, 4 g fiber, 3 g protein.
Daily value: 14% vitamin A, 6% vitamin C, 2% calcium, 9% iron.

APPLE-CRANBERRY STREUSEL PIE

Look for dried cranberries or cherries in specialty food stores or in the gourmet food aisle of your grocery store.

Pastry for Single-Crust Pie
(see recipe, page 50)
½ cup dried cranberries or dried tart cherries
6 large apples, peeled, cored, and sliced (6 cups)
¾ cup granulated sugar
3 tablespoons all-purpose flour
1 teaspoon apple pie spice
¼ teaspoon salt
⅓ cup half-and-half or light cream
⅓ cup all-purpose flour
⅓ cup finely chopped toasted pecans or walnuts
⅓ cup packed brown sugar
¼ teaspoon ground nutmeg
3 tablespoons butter or margarine
Vanilla Icing

Prepare pastry. Line pastry with a double thickness of foil. Bake in a 450° oven for 8 minutes. Remove foil. Bake for 5 to 6 minutes more or till golden. Cool on a wire rack. Reduce oven temperature to 375°.

For filling, pour enough boiling water over cranberries or cherries to cover. Let stand for 5 minutes; drain. Mix cranberries or cherries and apples; place in pastry shell. Combine granulated sugar, the 3 tablespoons flour, apple pie spice, and salt. Stir in half-and-half or light cream. Pour over fruit.

For topping, combine the ⅓ cup flour, nuts, brown sugar, and nutmeg. With a pastry blender, cut in butter or margarine till the pieces are the size of small peas. Sprinkle over filling.

Cover edge of pie with foil. Bake in a 375° oven for 25 minutes. Remove foil. Bake for 20 to 25 minutes more or till top is golden and fruit is tender. Cool pie for 45 minutes on a wire rack. Drizzle with Vanilla Icing. Serve warm or cool. Store any leftover pie, covered, in the refrigerator. Makes 8 servings.

Vanilla Icing: Combine ½ cup sifted *powdered sugar,* 1 teaspoon *milk,* and ¼ teaspoon *vanilla.* Stir in additional milk, 1 teaspoon at a time, till of drizzling consistency.

Nutrition fact per serving: 447 calories, 18 g total fat (9 g saturated fat), 15 mg cholesterol, 186 mg sodium, 72 g carbohydrate, 3 g fiber, 4 g protein.
Daily value: 5% vitamin A, 8% vitamin C, 3% calcium, 12% iron.

HONEY-FRUIT PIZZA

Pretty as a picture, this fresh-tasting masterpiece features a cookie crust, summer fruits, and a honey glaze.

¾ cup butter or margarine
⅓ cup sifted powdered sugar
2 cups all-purpose flour
2 tablespoons honey
1 tablespoon cornstarch
⅓ cup apple or orange juice
2 tablespoons currant or apple jelly
1 cup sliced strawberries
½ cup blueberries or raspberries
1 medium nectarine, pitted and sliced,
    or 1 medium peach, peeled, pitted,
    and sliced
½ cup seedless green or red grapes,
    halved

For crust, in a medium mixing bowl beat butter or margarine with an electric mixer on medium speed for 30 seconds. Beat in powdered sugar. Gradually add flour, beating till well mixed. Pat dough evenly into a greased 11- or 12-inch pizza pan. Bake in a 375° oven for 15 to 18 minutes or till golden brown. Cool in pan on a wire rack.

For glaze, in a small saucepan stir together honey and cornstarch. Stir in juice and jelly. Cook and stir over medium heat till mixture is thickened and bubbly. Cook 2 minutes more. Remove from heat. Cool 5 minutes (do not stir).

Spread *half* of the glaze onto the cooled crust. Arrange fruit over the crust. Spoon remaining glaze over fruit. Chill at least 30 minutes before serving. (Pizza may be chilled up to 6 hours before serving.) Makes 12 servings.

Nutrition facts per serving: 223 calories, 12 g total fat (7 g saturated fat), 31 mg cholesterol, 118 mg sodium, 28 g carbohydrate, 1 g fiber, 2 g protein.
Daily Value: 11% vitamin A, 15% vitamin C, 0% calcium, 7% iron.

STRAWBERRY TARTS

Serve these dainty tarts on your best china dessert plates lined with paper doilies.

½   cup butter or margarine, softened
1   3-ounce package cream cheese,
        softened
1   cup all-purpose flour
3   cups small whole strawberries
⅓   cup water
⅓   cup granulated sugar
1   tablespoon cornstarch
½   teaspoon finely shredded orange peel
        (optional)
    Several drops red food coloring
        (optional)
⅓   cup semisweet chocolate pieces
1   tcaspoon shortening
    Sweetened Whipped Cream (optional)
        (see recipe, page 116)
    Fresh mint (optional)

In a mixing bowl beat butter or margarine and cream cheese till well mixed. Stir in flour. Divide dough into 16 pieces. Press into 16 ungreased, 2½-inch muffin pan cups, pressing dough onto the bottom and halfway up sides. Bake in a 400° oven for 12 to 15 minutes or till golden. Cool on wire rack. Remove shells from muffin cups.

For glaze, in a blender container or food processor bowl combine *¾ cup* of the strawberries and the water. Cover and blend or process till smooth. If necessary, add enough additional water to make ¾ cup. In a small saucepan combine sugar and cornstarch. Stir in pureed strawberry mixture. Cook and stir over medium heat till mixture is thickened and bubbly. Cook and stir for 2 minutes more. Stir in orange peel and red food coloring, if desired. Cool for 10 minutes.

In a heavy small saucepan melt chocolate and shortening. Drizzle chocolate mixture into the bottom of the cooled pastry shells. Arrange whole strawberries, stem end down, in tart shells. Cut any large berries in half. Spoon glaze over berries. Chill for 1 to 2 hours. (After 2 hours, filling may begin to water out.) Serve with Sweetened Whipped Cream, and garnish with fresh mint, if desired. Makes 16.

Nutrition facts per serving: 140 calories, 9 g total fat (5 g saturated fat), 21 mg cholesterol, 75 mg sodium, 15 g carbohydrate, 1 g fiber, 2 g protein.
Daily Value: 7% vitamin A, 26% vitamin C, 1% calcium, 4% iron.

Glazed Raspberry Tarts: Prepare as directed above except substitute 3 cups *red raspberries* for the strawberries. If desired, press pureed raspberry mixture through a sieve to remove seeds.

Nutrition facts per serving: 144 calories, 9 g total fat (5 g saturated fat), 21 mg cholesterol, 83 mg sodium, 15 g carbohydrate, 1 g fiber, 2 g protein.
Daily Value: 9% vitamin A, 9% vitamin C, 1% calcium, 4% iron.

LEMON CURD PASTRY WITH MIXED BERRIES

Lemon curd is a tangy-sweet English spread. Look for a bottled version in the jam or specialty food section of the supermarket or in a gourmet food shop. You can substitute lemon pudding, although the flavor is milder.

½   of a 17¼-ounce package (1 sheet)
      frozen puff pastry
1   slightly beaten egg white
1   teaspoon water
      Coarse sugar or granulated sugar
⅔   cup lemon curd (at room
      temperature)
⅔   cup dairy sour cream
¼   teaspoon ground ginger
1   to 2 drops almond extract
3   cups fresh raspberries, blueberries,
      blackberries, and/or halved
      strawberries
¼   cup toasted sliced almonds
2   tablespoons honey

Let folded pastry thaw at room temperature for 20 minutes. On a lightly floured surface, unfold pastry and roll into a 15x10-inch rectangle. Cut from the long edges of the rectangle two ¾-inch-wide strips. From the short edges, cut two ¾-inch-wide strips. Set the 4 pastry strips aside.

Place the pastry rectangle onto an ungreased baking sheet. Combine egg white and water; brush onto the rectangle. Place the 4 pastry strips on the edges of rectangle, trimming to fit. Brush strips with egg white mixture; sprinkle with coarse or granulated sugar. Prick the bottom of the pastry several times with the tines of a fork.

Bake in a 375° oven for 20 to 25 minutes or till light brown. Remove from oven. Cool on a wire rack.

For filling, in a medium mixing bowl stir lemon curd till smooth. Stir together sour cream, ginger, and almond extract. Fold sour cream mixture into lemon curd.

Spread filling over cooled pastry. Cover and chill till serving time or up to 4 hours. Before serving, top with berries and almonds. Drizzle with honey. Serve immediately. Makes 8 servings.

Nutrition facts per serving: 267 calories, 16 g total fat (3 g saturated fat), 21 mg cholesterol, 149 mg sodium, 29 g carbohydrate, 2 g fiber, 4 g protein.
Daily Value: 5% vitamin A, 28% vitamin C, 3% calcium, 3% iron.

CROSTATA

This Italian dessert traditionally was made with dried fruits and preserves because fresh fruits were less available. Dried figs, apricot preserves, and fresh apples fill this updated version.

2   cups all-purpose flour
⅓   cup sugar
1½ teaspoons baking powder
⅓   cup butter or margarine
1   slightly beaten egg
⅓   cup milk
1   teaspoon vanilla
4   cups sliced, peeled apples
½   cup snipped dried figs
⅔   cup apricot or peach preserves
    Milk
    Sugar

In a medium mixing bowl stir together flour, ⅓ cup sugar, and baking powder. Cut in butter or margarine till mixture resembles coarse crumbs. Combine egg, ⅓ cup milk, and vanilla; add to flour mixture. Mix well. Shape into a ball.

On a lightly floured surface, knead dough gently for 10 to 12 strokes or till smooth. Wrap and chill *one-third* of the dough. Pat remaining dough onto the bottom and up sides of a 10- or 11-inch tart pan with removeable bottom.

Arrange apple slices and figs on pastry in tart pan. Stir preserves; cut up any large pieces of fruit. Spoon preserves evenly over fruit.

On a lightly floured surface, roll chilled pastry into a 9- or 10-inch circle. Cut into 12 wedges. Twist each wedge twice at narrow end; arrange in circle over apples and figs. Brush pastry with milk and sprinkle with sugar.

Bake in a 375° oven for 40 to 45 minutes or till fruit is tender. If necessary, to prevent overbrowning, cover loosely with foil the last 10 to 15 minutes of baking. Remove sides of pan before serving. Serve warm. Makes 8 to 10 servings.

Nutrition facts per serving: 361 calories, 9 g total fat (5 g saturated fat), 48 mg cholesterol, 164 mg sodium, 68 g carbohydrate, 3 g fiber, 5 g protein.
Daily Value: 9% vitamin A, 6% vitamin C, 9% calcium, 14% iron.

PASTRY STARS WITH FRUIT AND CREAM

Although you can cut the puff pastry into any shapes you wish, the star-shaped cutters make a festive dessert for Memorial Day or Fourth of July celebrations.

½   of a 17¼-ounce package (1 sheet)
     frozen puff pastry
2   cups sliced fresh strawberries
1½ cups fresh red raspberries
1   cup fresh blueberries
¼   cup granulated sugar
     Coarse sugar, red or blue sugar,
     or powdered sugar
½   cup whipping cream
¼   cup dairy sour cream
1   tablespoon granulated sugar

Thaw the puff pastry according to the package directions. Chill a medium mixing bowl and the beaters of an electric mixer. (A chilled bowl and beaters will help the cream to whip into peaks faster.)

In a large mixing bowl toss together all of the berries and the ¼ cup granulated sugar. Set aside.

On a lightly floured surface, unfold puff pastry. Using floured, star-shaped cutters of different sizes, cut pastry into stars.

Arrange star pastries on an ungreased baking sheet. Bake in a 350° oven about 15 minutes or till golden. Remove from baking sheet; cool slightly on a wire rack. Brush pastry stars lightly with *water;* sprinkle with coarse or colored sugar or powdered sugar.

Meanwhile, in the chilled bowl combine whipping cream, sour cream, and the 1 tablespoon granulated sugar. Beat with the chilled beaters of the electric mixer on low speed till soft peaks form.

To serve, pipe or spoon whipped cream mixture onto 6 dessert plates. Arrange the berries and pastry stars on plates. Serve immediately. Makes 6 servings.

Nutrition facts per serving: 359 calories, 23 g total fat (6 g saturated fat), 31 mg cholesterol, 168 mg sodium, 38 g carbohydrate, 3 g fiber, 3 g protein.
Daily Value: 11% vitamin A, 65% vitamin C, 3% calcium, 2% iron.

PEANUT BUTTER AND BANANA PIE

A creamy peanut butter filling and sliced bananas piled high in a peanutty crust make a yummy treat for kids and grown-ups alike.

¾ cup sugar
2 tablespoons cornstarch
1 cup milk
4 egg yolks, slightly beaten
½ cup creamy peanut butter
1 teaspoon vanilla
3 medium bananas
Peanut Crust
Sweetened Whipped Cream
    (see recipe, page 116)
1 medium banana
Peanuts (optional)

For filling, in a medium saucepan combine sugar and cornstarch. Gradually stir in milk. Cook and stir over medium heat till mixture is thickened and bubbly (6 to 8 minutes). Remove from heat. Gradually stir about *half* of the hot mixture into the beaten egg yolks. Return to saucepan. Bring to a gentle boil. Cook and stir for 2 minutes more. Remove from heat; stir in peanut butter and vanilla. Cool slightly (about 5 minutes).

Meanwhile, slice the 3 bananas. Arrange *half* of the banana slices in the bottom of the Peanut Crust. Top with *half* of the filling. Repeat layers. Cover and chill for 3 to 6 hours.

To serve, pipe or dollop Sweetened Whipped Cream around the edge of pie. Slice remaining banana. Arrange banana slices on pie. Sprinkle with peanuts, if desired. Makes 8 servings.

Peanut Crust: In a medium mixing bowl mix 1 cup *all-purpose flour,* 2 tablespoons *sugar,* and ⅓ cup finely chopped *peanuts.* Cut in ⅓ cup *shortening* till the pieces are the size of small peas. Sprinkle 3 to 4 tablespoons *cold water* over the flour mixture, 1 tablespoon at a time, gently tossing with a fork after each addition till all is moistened. Form dough into a ball. On a lightly floured surface, flatten dough with hands. Roll dough into a 12-inch circle. Ease into pie plate. Flute edges. Prick bottom and sides of pastry with a fork. Line pastry with a double thickness of foil. Bake in a 450° oven for 8 minutes. Remove foil. Bake for 5 to 6 minutes more or till lightly browned.

Nutrition facts per serving: 564 calories, 34 g total fat (12 g saturated fat), 150 mg cholesterol, 108 mg sodium, 58 g carbohydrate, 3 g fiber, 11 g protein.
Daily Value: 31% vitamin A, 9% vitamin C, 7% calcium, 10% iron.

BERRIES AND CREAM IN PHYLLO CUPS

Once unwrapped, sheets of phyllo dough quickly dry out. Allow frozen phyllo dough to thaw while it is still wrapped and keep the open stack covered with a slightly moistened cloth while you prepare the phyllo cups.

4   sheets frozen phyllo dough (about 17x12-inch rectangles), thawed
2   tablespoons butter or margarine, melted
1   8-ounce package cream cheese
3   tablespoons orange marmalade, snipped
1¼   cup fresh red raspberries
1¼   cup fresh blueberries
3   tablespoons orange marmalade, snipped (optional)

Grease twelve 2½-inch muffin cups; set aside.

Unfold phyllo dough. Place 1 sheet on a flat surface. Brush lightly with some of the melted butter or margarine. Top with a second sheet; brush again. Cut into twelve 4-inch squares. Place a square in each muffin cup. Make a second stack with 2 more sheets of phyllo and remaining butter or margarine. Cut into twelve 4-inch squares. Place a square in each muffin cup so that all 8 corners of phyllo show.

Bake in a 375° oven about 4 minutes or till phyllo is lightly browned and crisp. Cool in pans on wire rack. Carefully remove shells from muffin cups.

In a small mixing bowl beat the cream cheese and 3 tablespoons snipped marmalade till well combined. Spoon a rounded tablespoon into each phyllo cup. Chill for up to 4 hours before serving. Top with raspberries and blueberries. If desired, melt remaining marmalade in a small saucepan over low heat, stirring constantly; drizzle over berries. Makes 12 servings.

Nutrition facts per serving: 130 calories, 9 g total fat (5 g saturated fat), 26 mg cholesterol, 108 mg sodium, 11 g carbohydrate, 1 g fiber, 2 g protein.
Daily Value: 10% vitamin A, 9% vitamin C, 1% calcium, 3% iron.

CRANBERRY-APPLE TART

Sweet apples, tangy cranberries, and a buttery oat topping fill a brandy-laced pastry in this homespun tart.

1¼ cups all-purpose flour
2 tablespoons sugar
1 teaspoon baking powder
¼ teaspoon salt
⅓ cup butter or margarine
1 egg yolk, beaten
2 tablespoons brandy or milk
2 cups sliced peeled apples
1 cup cranberries
¾ cup sugar
¼ cup rolled oats
2 tablespoons all-purpose flour
½ teaspoon ground cinnamon
2 tablespoons butter or margarine
Dairy sour cream (optional)
Ground cinnamon (optional)
Whole cranberries (optional)
Sugar (optional)

For crust, in a medium mixing bowl stir together 1¼ cups flour, 2 tablespoons sugar, baking powder, and salt. Cut in ⅓ cup butter or margarine till mixture resembles coarse crumbs. Combine egg yolk and brandy or milk; add to dry ingredients and mix well. Press mixture onto the bottom and 1 inch up the sides of a 9x1½-inch round baking pan.

Arrange apple slices over crust. Sprinkle with cranberries.

In a medium mixing bowl combine ¾ cup sugar, rolled oats, 2 tablespoons flour, and cinnamon. Cut in 2 tablespoons butter or margarine till mixture resembles coarse crumbs. Sprinkle over apples and cranberries.

Bake in a 350° oven for 40 to 45 minutes or till apples are tender. Cool slightly. Serve warm. (Or, place cooled tart in a 350° oven for 5 to 10 minutes or till warm. Serve immediately.) Top with sour cream and sprinkle with ground cinnamon, if desired. Garnish with whole cranberries rolled in sugar, if desired. Makes 6 to 8 servings.

Nutrition facts per serving: 397 calories, 15 g total fat (9 g saturated fat), 73 mg cholesterol, 293 mg sodium, 60 g carbohydrate, 3 g fiber, 4 g protein.
Daily Value: 18% vitamin A, 7% vitamin C, 6% calcium, 11% iron.

PEACH-PRALINE COBBLER

Pecan-swirled biscuits make a tasty topping for this juicy cobbler.

  8 cups sliced, peeled, fresh or
        frozen peaches
  1 cup granulated sugar
  1 cup water
  2 tablespoons cornstarch
  1 teaspoon ground cinnamon
  ¾ cup packed brown sugar
  ¼ cup butter or margarine, melted
1½ cups chopped pecans
  2 cups all-purpose flour
  2 teaspoons granulated sugar
  2 teaspoons baking powder
  ½ teaspoon baking soda
  ½ teaspoon salt
  ½ cup shortening
  ¾ cup buttermilk
        Half-and-half or light cream
          (optional)

Thaw frozen peach slices, if using. *Do not drain.*

In a Dutch oven combine peaches, 1 cup granulated sugar, water, cornstarch, and cinnamon. Cook and stir till mixture is thickened and bubbly. Keep warm.

Meanwhile, for pecan filling, stir together brown sugar and melted butter or margarine. Add pecans; toss to mix. Set aside.

For dough, in a large mixing bowl stir together flour, 2 teaspoons granulated sugar, baking powder, baking soda, and salt. Cut in shortening till mixture resembles coarse crumbs. Make a well in the center; add buttermilk. Stir just till dough clings together.

Turn dough out onto a lightly floured surface. Knead gently for 10 to 12 strokes. Roll dough into a 12x8-inch rectangle; spread with pecan filling. Roll up from one of the long sides. Cut into twelve 1-inch-thick slices.

Transfer hot peach mixture to a shallow 3-quart baking dish. Place slices, cut side down, on top of the hot peach mixture. Bake in a 400° oven for 25 to 30 minutes or till topping is golden. Serve warm with half-and-half or light cream, if desired. Makes 12 servings.

Nutrition facts per serving: 438 calories, 22 g total fat (5 g saturated fat), 11 mg cholesterol, 261 mg sodium, 60 g carbohydrate, 3 g fiber, 4 g protein.
Daily Value: 9% vitamin A, 8% vitamin C, 8% calcium, 11% iron.

CHERRY-BERRY CRISP

Pit fresh cherries using either a commercially made cherry pitter or the tip of a knife.

4   cups fresh or frozen pitted tart
      red cherries
1   cup fresh or frozen blueberries
½   cup granulated sugar
3   tablespoons all-purpose flour
½   cup packed brown sugar
¼   cup all-purpose flour
¼   cup butter or margarine
½   cup rolled oats
½   cup chopped pecans or walnuts
      Vanilla or cinnamon ice cream
        (optional)

Thaw frozen cherries and blueberries, if using. *Do not drain.*

In a 2-quart square baking dish combine cherries and blueberries. Stir in granulated sugar and 3 tablespoons flour.

For topping, in a medium mixing bowl combine brown sugar and ¼ cup flour. Cut in butter or margarine till mixture resembles coarse crumbs. Stir in oats and nuts. Sprinkle topping over cherry mixture.

Bake in a 375° oven about 40 minutes or till filling is bubbly and topping is golden. Serve warm and, if desired, with vanilla or cinnamon ice cream. Makes 6 servings.

Nutrition facts per serving: 368 calories, 15 g total fat (5 g saturated fat), 20 mg cholesterol, 87 mg sodium, 60 g carbohydrate, 3 g fiber, 4 g protein.
Daily Value: 20% vitamin A, 14% vitamin C, 3% calcium, 10% iron.

CHOCOLATE AND PEAR BREAD PUDDING

Cream cheese and semisweet chocolate pieces make an exceptionally rich custard in this fruity bread pudding.

1   8-ounce package cream cheese,
       softened
⅔   cup sugar
1   teaspoon finely shredded lemon peel
1   teaspoon vanilla
¼   teaspoon ground nutmeg
¼   teaspoon ground cinnamon
4   eggs
1½   cups milk, half-and-half, or
       light cream
3   cups dry bread cubes
       (about 4 slices bread)
4   medium pears, peeled, cored, and
       thinly sliced (2 cups)
⅓   cup miniature semisweet chocolate
       pieces
1   teaspoon sugar
⅛   teaspoon ground nutmeg
⅛   teaspoon ground cinnamon

In a large mixing bowl beat cream cheese, the ⅔ cup sugar, lemon peel, vanilla, the ¼ teaspoon nutmeg, and the ¼ teaspoon cinnamon with an electric mixer on low speed till smooth. Beat in eggs, 1 at a time, beating just till combined after each addition. With a large spoon, stir in milk, half-and-half, or light cream; bread; pears; and chocolate pieces. Pour mixture into an ungreased 2-quart square baking dish, stirring gently to distribute chocolate pieces.

In a small mixing bowl combine the 1 teaspoon sugar, the ⅛ teaspoon nutmeg, and the ⅛ teaspoon cinnamon. Sprinkle over pear mixture. Place dish in a 13x9x2-inch baking pan; set on oven rack. Pour hot water into the 13x9x2-inch baking pan to a depth of 1 inch. Bake in a 350° oven about 45 minutes or till a knife inserted near the center comes out clean. Serve warm or cool. Makes 9 servings.

Nutrition facts per serving: 306 calories, 14 g total fat (7 g saturated fat), 126 mg cholesterol, 176 mg sodium, 39 g carbohydrate, 2 g fiber, 8 g protein.
Daily Value: 17% vitamin A, 6% vitamin C, 8% calcium, 8% iron.

GINGER CUSTARD WITH PLUM SAUCE

For a rosy red sauce, choose a variety of plums with red skin, such as Red Beaut, Ace, or Queen Ann.

4   eggs, slightly beaten
2   cups milk
½   cup sugar
1   teaspoon vanilla
½   teaspoon ground ginger
6   fresh medium plums, pitted and
      coarsely chopped (2½ cups)
⅓   cup sugar
1   tablespoon lemon juice
1   tablespoon water
1½ teaspoons cornstarch
½   teaspoon vanilla

Combine eggs, milk, the ½ cup sugar, the 1 teaspoon vanilla, and the ginger. Beat till well combined but not foamy. Place six 6-ounce custard cups in a large shallow baking pan on oven rack. Pour egg mixture into custard cups. Pour hot water into pan around custard cups to reach halfway up sides of custard cups.

Bake in a 350° oven for 30 to 35 minutes or till a knife inserted near centers comes out clean. Remove cups from water. Cool on a wire rack at least 20 minutes.

Meanwhile, for plum sauce, in a medium saucepan combine chopped plums, the ⅓ cup sugar, and lemon juice. Bring to boiling. Reduce heat; cover and simmer about 8 minutes or till plums are tender. Stir together water and cornstarch. Add to plum mixture. Cook and stir till thickened and bubbly. Cook and stir for 2 minutes more. Remove from heat. Stir in the ½ teaspoon vanilla.

To serve, unmold custards onto dessert plates. Spoon sauce over custards. Makes 6 servings.

Nutrition facts per serving: 241 calories, 5 g total fat (2 g saturated fat), 148 mg cholesterol, 83 mg sodium, 42 g carbohydrate, 1 g fiber, 7 g protein.
Daily Value: *13% vitamin A, 13% vitamin C, 9% calcium, 4% iron.*

APPLE-DATE PUDDING

The tastes of autumn come alive in this homespun dessert featuring chunks of tart apples baked in a spiced custard and topped with a rich caramel sauce.

2 cups chopped baking apples
       (2 to 3 medium)
2 slices whole wheat bread, cut into
       ½-inch cubes
½ cup snipped dates or raisins
4 eggs
2 12-ounce cans (3 cups)
       evaporated milk
½ cup sugar
¼ cup all-purpose flour
2 teaspoons vanilla
   Ground cinnamon
   Ground nutmeg
   Caramel Sauce

In a 2-quart square baking dish combine apples, bread cubes, and dates or raisins. Toss to mix.

In a large mixing bowl beat together eggs, evaporated milk, sugar, flour, and vanilla. Pour over apple mixture in baking dish. Sprinkle with cinnamon and nutmeg.

Bake in a 350° oven for 50 to 55 minutes or until a knife inserted near the center comes out clean. Cool slightly. Serve with warm Caramel Sauce. Makes 8 servings.

Caramel Sauce: In a heavy saucepan stir together ½ cup packed *brown sugar* and 1 tablespoon *cornstarch*. Stir in ¼ cup *water*. Stir in ⅓ cup *half-and-half or light cream* and 2 tablespoons *light corn syrup*. Cook and stir till bubbly (mixture may appear curdled). Cook and stir for 2 minutes more. Remove from heat. Stir in 1 tablespoon *butter or margarine* and ½ teaspoon *vanilla*. Serve warm.

Nutrition facts per serving: 381 calories, 12 g total fat (6 g saturated fat), 139 mg cholesterol, 181 mg sodium, 60 g carbohydrate, 2 g fiber, 11 g protein.
Daily Value: 13% vitamin A, 7% vitamin C, 22% calcium, 10% iron.

PEAR-BUTTERSCOTCH BETTY

Layers of sliced pears, whole wheat bread cubes, and a yummy butterscotch sauce bake together in this family-style dessert.

⅓ cup butter or margarine
¾ cup packed brown sugar
¼ cup half-and-half or light cream
2 tablespoons light corn syrup
⅛ teaspoon salt
1 teaspoon ground cinnamon
4 cups soft whole wheat bread cubes
5 ripe medium pears, peeled and thinly
    sliced
2 tablespoons butter or margarine,
    melted
    Sweetened Whipped Cream
    (see recipe, page 116)

For sauce, in a medium saucepan melt ⅓ cup butter or margarine. Add brown sugar, half-and-half or light cream, corn syrup, and salt. Bring to boiling, stirring constantly. Remove from heat. Stir in cinnamon. Cool slightly.

In a greased 1½-quart casserole place *one-third* of the bread cubes. Top with *half* of the sliced pears. Spoon *half* of the sauce over all. Repeat layers. Toss remaining bread cubes with 2 tablespoons melted butter or margarine. Sprinkle over layers.

Bake in a 350° oven for 40 minutes. Serve warm with Sweetened Whipped Cream. Makes 6 servings.

Nutrition facts per serving: 539 calories, 31 g total fat (19 g saturated fat), 96 mg cholesterol, 380 mg sodium, 65 g carbohydrate., 7 g fiber, 4 g protein
Daily Value: 31% vitamin A, 9% vitamin C, 8% calcium, 14% iron

PEACH AND ALMOND CRISP

Tuck juicy summer peaches under a blanket of crisp buttery almond streusel for this tantalizing dessert.

8	cups sliced peeled peaches or nectarines or frozen unsweetened peach slices
⅓	cup granulated sugar
¼	cup all-purpose flour
½	teaspoon ground cinnamon
¼	teaspoon ground nutmeg
⅛	teaspoon ground ginger
¼	cup peach nectar or orange juice
⅔	cup packed brown sugar
½	cup rolled oats
½	cup toasted sliced almonds
½	cup all-purpose flour
3	tablespoons granulated sugar
½	cup butter or margarine, cut up
	Vanilla ice cream (optional)

Thaw frozen peach slices, if using. *Do not drain.*

In a large mixing bowl stir together the ⅓ cup granulated sugar, the ¼ cup flour, cinnamon, nutmeg, and ginger. Add peaches or nectarines and peach nectar or orange juice. Toss gently to coat. Transfer filling to a 3-quart rectangular baking dish.

For topping, in a medium mixing bowl stir together brown sugar, oats, almonds, the ½ cup flour, and the 3 tablespoons granulated sugar. Using a pastry blender or 2 forks, cut in butter or margarine till mixture resembles coarse crumbs. Sprinkle topping over peach mixture in baking dish.

Bake in a 400° oven for 30 to 35 minutes or till peaches are tender and topping is golden. Serve warm or at room temperature and, if desired, with ice cream. Makes 12 servings.

Nutrition facts per serving: 253 calories, 10 g total fat (5 g saturated fat), 20 mg cholesterol, 81 mg sodium, 40 g carbohydrate, 3g fiber, 3 g protein.
Daily Value: 13% vitamin A, 12% vitamin C, 3% calcium, 7% iron.

APRICOT BREAD PUDDING

Chunks of golden apricots or peaches brighten this classic bread pudding.

8 1-inch-thick slices French or
   Italian bread
2 tablespoons butter or margarine,
   softened
2 cups chopped, pitted apricots or
   chopped, pitted, peeled peaches
5 eggs
2 cups milk
½ cup sugar
⅓ cup apricot or peach nectar
1 teaspoon vanilla
½ teaspoon ground cinnamon

Arrange bread slices on a baking sheet. Bake in a 450° oven for 3 to 5 minutes or till lightly toasted. Cool. Spread slices with butter or margarine. Cut into 1-inch cubes.

In a greased 2-quart rectangular baking dish combine bread cubes and apricots or peaches. Toss to mix.

In a large mixing bowl beat together eggs, milk, sugar, apricot or peach nectar, vanilla, and cinnamon. Pour over fruit mixture in baking dish.

Bake in a 325° oven about 50 minutes or until a knife inserted near the center comes out clean. Cool on a wire rack about 20 minutes. Serve warm. Makes 8 servings.

Nutrition facts per serving: 240 calories, 8 g total fat (3 g saturated fat), 145 mg cholesterol, 220 mg sodium, 34 g carbohydrate, 2 g fiber, 9 g protein.
Daily Value: 25% vitamin A, 14% vitamin C, 8% calcium, 10% iron.

PLUM COBBLER

Leave the peels on the plums. The filling will be more colorful, retain more vitamins, and be faster for the cook to fix.

1   cup sugar
3   tablespoons cornstarch
2   pounds fresh plums, pitted and
    quartered
⅓   cup water
1   tablespoon lemon juice
⅔   cup all-purpose flour
⅓   cup yellow cornmeal
¼   cup sugar
1   teaspoon baking powder
¼   teaspoon salt
1   egg, slightly beaten
⅓   cup milk
3   tablespoons butter or margarine,
    melted
    Vanilla ice cream (optional)

For filling, in a 3-quart saucepan combine the 1 cup sugar and cornstarch. Add plums, water, and lemon juice. Cook and stir over medium heat till mixture is thickened and bubbly. Keep warm.

In a medium mixing bowl stir together flour, cornmeal, the ¼ cup sugar, baking powder, and salt. Add egg, milk, and butter or margarine, stirring just till moistened.

Pour the hot filling into a 2-quart square baking dish. Drop dough by spoonfuls over the hot filling. Bake in a 400° oven for 20 to 25 minutes or till topping is light brown. Cool slightly on a wire rack. Serve warm and, if desired, with ice cream. Makes 8 servings.

Nutrition facts per serving: 303 calories, 6 g total fat (3 g saturated fat), 39 mg cholesterol, 170 mg sodium, 61 g carbohydrate, 3 g fiber, 4 g protein.
***Daily Value:** 9% vitamin A, 19% vitamin C, 5% calcium, 6% iron.*

PEACH CLAFOUTI WITH CITRUS SAUCE

Clafouti (cla FOO ti) is a French dessert made by topping a layer of fresh fruit with a batter. It's a cinch to make and sweetly satisfying to eat.

2 medium peaches, peeled, pitted,
   and sliced
2 tablespoons sugar
2 cups evaporated milk
3 eggs
¼ cup all-purpose flour
3 tablespoons sugar
½ teaspoon almond extract
½ teaspoon vanilla
  Dash salt
  Citrus Sauce

In an 9x1-inch round baking pan combine peaches and the 2 tablespoons sugar. Set aside.

In a blender container combine evaporated milk, eggs, flour, the 3 tablespoons sugar, almond extract, vanilla, and salt. Cover and blend for 15 seconds. Pour over peaches in dish.

Bake in a 375° oven for 40 to 45 minutes or till a knife inserted near the center comes out clean. Cool slightly. Spoon into bowls. Serve warm with Citrus Sauce. Makes 4 servings.

Citrus Sauce: In a small saucepan combine ⅓ cup *sugar* and 2 teaspoons *cornstarch*. Stir in ⅔ cup *water*. Cook and stir over medium heat till thickened and bubbly. Cook and stir for 2 minutes more. Remove from heat. Stir in 2 tablespoons *orange juice* and 1 tablespoon *lemon juice*.

Nutrition facts per serving: 408 calories, 13 g total fat (7 g saturated fat), 196 mg cholesterol, 216 mg sodium, 58 g carbohydrate, 1 g fiber, 14 g protein.
Daily Value: 18% vitamin A, 18% vitamin C, 29% calcium, 8% iron.

FRESH BERRY CRISP

This juicy crisp, featuring summer's most luscious berries, makes the perfect finale to a backyard cookout.

2 cups fresh or frozen blackberries
1 cup fresh or frozen red or black
     raspberries
1 cup fresh or frozen blueberries
½ cup sugar
2 tablespoons cornstarch
½ cup apple juice or pear nectar
1 teaspoon finely shredded lemon peel
⅔ cup all-purpose flour
⅔ cup rolled oats
2 tablespoons sugar
¼ teaspoon ground nutmeg
½ cup butter or margarine
⅓ cup finely chopped walnuts or pecans
   Fresh mint (optional)
   Fresh raspberries or blackberries
     (optional)
   Ice cream or frozen yogurt (optional)

Thaw frozen blackberries, raspberries, and blueberries, if using. *Do not drain.*

In a 2-quart square baking dish combine blackberries, raspberries, and blueberries. Toss gently to mix. Set aside.

In a small saucepan stir together the ½ cup sugar and the cornstarch. Stir in apple juice or pear nectar. Cook and stir till mixture is thickened and bubbly. Stir in lemon peel. Pour over berries in baking dish; stir gently to mix.

For topping, in a medium mixing bowl combine flour, oats, the 2 tablespoons sugar, and nutmeg. Cut in butter or margarine till mixture resembles coarse crumbs. Stir in nuts. Sprinkle topping over berry mixture.

Bake in a 350° oven for 35 to 40 minutes or till berries are bubbly and topping is golden. Serve warm. Garnish with fresh mint and additional fresh berries, if desired. Serve with ice cream or frozen yogurt, if desired. Makes 6 servings.

Nutrition facts per serving: 407 calories, 20 g total fat (10 g saturated fat), 41 mg cholesterol, 159 mg sodium, 55 g carbohydrate, 6 g fiber, 5 g protein.
Daily Value: 15% vitamin A, 19% vitamin C, 3% calcium, 11% iron.

PEACH-PECAN ICE CREAM

Toasting the pecans intensifies their flavor and helps keep them crisp.

3 cups half-and-half or light cream
1½ cups sugar
1 tablespoon vanilla
3 cups whipping cream
4 cups finely chopped, peeled peaches
    or one 16-ounce package frozen
    unsweetened peach slices, thawed
    and finely chopped
½ cup chopped toasted pecans
    Peach slices (optional)

In a very large mixing bowl combine half-and-half or light cream, sugar, and vanilla. Stir till sugar is dissolved. Stir in whipping cream. Then stir in peaches and toasted pecans.

Freeze in a 4- or 5-quart ice-cream freezer according to manufacturer's directions. Garnish with peach slices, if desired. Makes 2 quarts (16 servings).

Nutrition facts per serving: 329 calories, 24 g total fat, (14 g saturated fat), 78 mg cholesterol, 35 mg sodium, 28 g carbohydrate, 1 g fiber, 3 g protein.
Daily Value: 27% vitamin A, 4% vitamin C, 6% calcium, 1% iron.

FROZEN BLACKBERRY MOUSSE

For this refreshing summer treat, you simply mix fresh berries with whipped cream and freeze the mixture in individual portions.

2 cups fresh blackberries or ½ of a 16-
  ounce package frozen blackberries
1 cup whipping cream
½ cup sugar
½ teaspoon vanilla
  Chocolate or White Filigree Leaves
  (optional)
  Fresh red raspberries or blackberries
  (optional)

Thaw berries, if frozen.

Line eight 2½-inch muffin pan cups with foil or paper bake cups. Place the blackberries in a bowl. Crush the berries slightly. Set aside.

In a large mixing bowl combine whipping cream, sugar, and vanilla. Beat with an electric mixer on medium to high speed just till soft peaks form. Fold in crushed berries. Spoon into lined muffin cups. Freeze till firm.

To serve, remove bake cups. Place on dessert plates. Garnish with Chocolate or White Filigree Leaves and raspberries or blackberries, if desired. Makes 8 servings.

Chocolate or White Filigree Leaves: Line a large baking sheet with waxed paper; set aside. In a heavy small saucepan melt 2 ounces *chocolate- or vanilla-flavored candy coating* over low heat. Using a small spoon, drizzle candy coating mixture onto the waxed-paper-lined baking sheet in lacy leaf shapes. Let stand until set.

Nutrition facts per serving: 171 calories, 11 g total fat (7 g saturated fat), 41 mg cholesterol, 11 mg sodium, 18 g carbohydrate, 2 g fiber, 1 g protein.
Daily Value: *13% vitamin A, 12%vitamin C, 2% calcium, 1% iron*

MELON SORBET

A hint of orange enhances the sweetness of whichever melon you choose—watermelon, cantaloupe, or honeydew melon.

1½ cups water
  1 cup sugar
  5 cups cubed, seeded watermelon,
       cantaloupe, or honeydew melon
  2 teaspoons finely shredded orange peel
 ½ cup orange juice
     Fresh mint (optional)

In a medium saucepan combine water and sugar. Cook over medium-low heat till sugar dissolves. Cover and chill till cold.

In a large mixing bowl combine melon, orange peel, orange juice, and chilled sugar mixture. Place *one-third to one-half* of the melon mixture in a blender or food processor. Cover and blend or process till smooth, stopping and scraping sides as necessary. Place pureed mixture in another bowl. Repeat with remaining melon mixture.

Freeze in an ice-cream freezer according to manufacturer's directions. (Or, pour the mixture into a 9x9x2-inch baking pan. Freeze about 3 hours or till frozen around the edges. Spoon into a large chilled bowl. Beat with an electric mixer on high speed till smooth, but not melted. Return to pan. Cover and freeze several hours or overnight.)

To serve, let stand at room temperature for 5 to10 minutes. Scoop into dessert dishes. Garnish with mint, if desired. Makes 8 servings.

Nutrition facts per serving: 136 calories, 0 g total fat (0 g saturated fat), 0 mg cholesterol, 3 mg sodium, 34 g carbohydrate, 1 g fiber, 1 g protein.
Daily Value: 3% vitamin A, 30% vitamin C, 0% calcium, 1% iron.

STRAWBERRY ICE CREAM

Always a favorite, this strawberry ice cream is velvety smooth, extra rich, and totally creamy. Scoop it into cones for a summertime treat.

2   cups sugar
2   envelopes unflavored gelatin
6   cups half-and-half or light cream
6   beaten eggs
2   cups whipping cream
3   tablespoons vanilla
      Several drops red food coloring
         (optional)
3   to 4 cups sliced strawberries
¼   cup sugar

In a large saucepan combine the 2 cups sugar and the gelatin. Stir in half-and-half or light cream. Cook and stir over medium heat till mixture almost boils and sugar dissolves. Stir about *1 cup* of the hot mixture into the beaten eggs; return all of the mixture to the saucepan. Cook and stir for 2 minutes more. *Do not boil.* Stir in whipping cream, vanilla, and, if desired, red food coloring. Cool.

In a small mixing bowl combine sliced strawberries and the ¼ cup sugar. Use a pastry blender or potato masher to slightly crush the strawberries; stir into cooled custard.

Freeze in a 4- or 5-quart ice-cream freezer according to manufacturer's directions. Makes about 3 quarts (24 servings).

Nutrition facts per serving: 251 calories, 16 g total fat (9 g saturated fat), 103 mg cholesterol, 49 mg sodium, 24 g carbohydrate, 0 g fiber, 4 g protein.
Daily Value: *19% vitamin A, 19% vitamin C, 7% calcium, 2% iron.*

TROPICAL TRIFLE

This exotic trifle features fresh mangoes and pineapple. For a more traditional trifle, substitute 3 cups peeled, sliced peaches and 2 cups raspberries.

3	eggs
1¼	cups milk
¼	cup sugar
1	teaspoon vanilla
1	3-ounce package ladyfingers or 12 ladyfingers, split
3	tablespoons light rum or pineapple juice
2	ripe mangoes, peeled, seeded, and cubed
2	cups cubed fresh pineapple
1	cup whipping cream
2	tablespoons sugar
½	teaspoon vanilla
2	tablespoons coconut, toasted

For custard, in a heavy medium saucepan lightly beat eggs just till mixed. Stir in milk and the ¼ cup sugar. Cook and stir over medium heat till mixture just coats a metal spoon, about 7 minutes. Remove from heat; stir in the 1 teaspoon vanilla. Pour custard into a bowl. Cover surface with plastic wrap. Let stand 30 minutes or till cool.

Tear ladyfingers into 1-inch pieces. In a 2-quart clear glass serving bowl arrange *half* of the ladyfingers. Sprinkle with *half* of the rum or pineapple juice. Top with *half* of the mangoes and *half* of the pineapple. Pour *half* of the custard over the fruit. Repeat layers. Cover and chill in the refrigerator for 4 to 6 hours.

Just before serving, in a chilled small mixing bowl combine whipping cream, the 2 tablespoons sugar, and the ½ teaspoon vanilla. Beat with an electric mixer on medium speed till soft peaks form. Pipe or spread whipped cream over trifle. Sprinkle with coconut. Serves 8.

Nutrition facts per serving: 298 calories, 15 g total fat (8 g saturated fat), 162 mg cholesterol, 73 mg sodium, 33 g carbohydrate, 2 g fiber, 6 g protein.
Daily Value: 41% vitamin A, 35% vitamin C, 7% calcium, 6% iron.

CITRUS GRANITA

For optimal flavor, use freshly squeezed fruit juices in this zingy ice.

2½ cups water
1¼ cups sugar
 1 cup orange juice
¾ cup lemon juice
½ cup grapefruit juice
¼ cup lime juice
    **Thin lemon and lime wedges
      (optional)**

In a large saucepan stir together water and sugar. Cook over medium heat till boiling. Remove from heat and cool to lukewarm. Strain the orange juice, lemon juice, grapefruit juice, and lime juice through a fine strainer. Stir fruit juices into the syrup.

Pour the juice mixture into a 13x9x2-inch baking pan; place in the freezer. Freeze for 45 to 60 minutes or till mixture is slushy on the edges. Stir mixture. Freeze 10 minutes more; stir the mixture, scraping frozen mixture off the bottom and sides of pan. Continue freezing, stirring the mixture every 30 minutes or till all of the mixture is slushy (this will take 3 to 3½ hours). Stir well and pour into a freezer container. Cover and freeze several hours or overnight.

To serve, let stand at room temperature for 5 to 10 minutes. Scoop into chilled dessert glasses. Garnish with lemon and lime wedges, if desired. Makes 8 servings.

Nutrition facts per serving: 149 calories, 0 g total fat (0 g saturated fat), 0 mg cholesterol, 3 mg sodium, 39 g carbohydrate., 0 g fiber, 0 g protein.
Daily Value: 0% vitamin A, 56% vitamin C, 0% calcium, 0% iron.

Citrus Spritzer: Spoon Citrus Granita into 8 tall glasses. Add *club soda* to fill.

Nutrition facts per serving: 149 calories, 0 g total fat (0 g saturated fat), 0 mg cholesterol, 27 mg sodium, 39 g carbohydrate., 0 g fiber, 0 g protein.
Daily Value: 0% vitamin A, 56% vitamin C, 1% calcium, 0% iron.

STRAWBERRY AND COFFEE COUPE

A coupe (COOP) is a French dessert featuring fruit and ice cream. This super easy coupe features marinated berries spooned over coffee ice cream that's swirled with sour cream and coffee liqueur.

1   **pint coffee ice cream**
1   **cup dairy sour cream or plain yogurt**
2   **tablespoons coffee liqueur**
2   **cups halved fresh strawberries**
1   **tablespoon coffee liqueur**
4   **to 6 teaspoons sugar**
    Fresh whole strawberries (optional)

In a medium mixing bowl stir ice cream with a spoon to soften. Stir in sour cream or yogurt and the 2 tablespoons liqueur. Cover and return to freezer for 4 to 5 hours or till firm.

In a small mixing bowl combine strawberries, the 1 tablespoon liqueur, and sugar. Cover and chill for at least 2 hours.

To serve, scoop ice cream into dessert dishes or goblets. Top with strawberry mixture. Serve with additional fresh strawberries, if desired. Makes 4 servings.

Nutrition facts per serving: 338 calories, 20 g total fat (12 g saturated fat), 55 mg cholesterol, 86 mg sodium, 33 g carbohydrate, 1g fiber, 5 g protein.
***Daily Value:** 21% vitamin A, 71% vitamin C, 13% calcium, 2% iron.*

PEACH SORBET

Serve this sorbet, ripe with the rich flavor of peaches, for a sophisticated dessert.

1¼ pounds fresh peaches, peeled, pitted, and cut up (2½ cups) or one 16-ounce package frozen unsweetened peach slices, thawed slightly
3 tablespoons lemon juice
1 cup sugar
1 cup boiling water
1 cup dry white wine
1½ teaspoons finely shredded orange peel
Edible violets (optional)

In a blender container or food processor bowl combine peaches and lemon juice; cover and blend or process till smooth.

In a large mixing bowl stir together sugar and boiling water till sugar is dissolved. Stir in peach mixture, wine, and orange peel. Pour into a 9x9x2-inch baking pan.

Cover and freeze for 3 to 4 hours or till firm. Break into chunks; transfer to a chilled large mixing bowl. Beat with an electric mixer on medium to high speed till smooth. Return to pan; cover. Freeze for several hours or till firm. Let stand for 20 minutes at room temperature before scooping into dessert dishes. Garnish with violets, if desired. Makes 8 servings.

Nutrition facts per serving: 141 calories, 0 g total fat (0 g saturated fat), 0 mg cholesterol, 3 mg sodium, 32 g carbohydrate, 1 g fiber, 0 g protein.
Daily Value: 2% vitamin A, 11% vitamin C, 0% calcium, 1% iron.

FROSTY CHOCOLATE-CHERRY YOGURT

Vanilla yogurt swirled with dark sweet cherries and semisweet chocolate pieces makes a cool, creamy, and ultimately scrumptious alternative to ice cream.

2 **16-ounce cartons (3½ cups) vanilla yogurt (no gelatin added)***
2½ **cups fresh or frozen pitted dark sweet cherries**
⅓ **cup milk**
⅓ **cup light corn syrup**
½ **cup miniature semisweet chocolate pieces**
   Fresh dark sweet cherries (optional)

In a blender container or food processor bowl combine yogurt, *1 cup* of the cherries, milk, and corn syrup. Cover and blend or process till almost smooth. If using a food processor, process half at a time.

Freeze mixture in a 2-quart ice-cream freezer according to manufacturer's directions till almost firm. Add remaining 1½ cups cherries and chocolate pieces; continue to freeze as directed till firm. Serve with additional fresh cherries, if desired. Makes 6 cups (12 servings).

***Note:** Yogurt without gelatin gives this dessert a better texture when frozen. The ingredient list on the carton will tell you if a refrigerated yogurt contains gelatin.

Nutrition facts per serving: 299 calories, 8 g total fat (2 g saturated fat), 9 mg cholesterol, 107 mg sodium, 55 g carbohydrate, 1 g fiber, 8 g protein.
***Daily Value:** 5% vitamin A, 7% vitamin C, 19% calcium, 9% iron.*

RASPBERRY AND CREAM TORTE

Orange-scented sponge cake layers with raspberries and sweetened whipped cream make this torte a festive finale for any meal.

1¼ cups all-purpose flour
  1 teaspoon baking powder
 ¼ teaspoon salt
  4 egg yolks
  1 teaspoon finely shredded orange peel
    (set aside)
 ⅓ cup orange juice
 ½ cup sugar
  4 egg whites
 ½ teaspoon cream of tartar
 ½ cup sugar
1½ cups whipping cream
  3 tablespoons granulated sugar
1½ teaspoons vanilla
  2 cups fresh red raspberries or
    sliced strawberries
  1 2-ounce square white baking bar,
    cut up and melted
    Fresh red raspberries (optional)
    White Filigree Leaves (optional)
    (see recipe, page 99)

Stir together flour, baking powder and salt; set aside. In a medium mixing bowl beat egg yolks with an electric mixer on high speed 6 minutes or till thick and lemon-colored. Add orange juice. Beat on low speed 30 seconds. Gradually add ½ cup sugar, beating on medium speed 5 minutes or till sugar is almost dissolved. Stir in orange peel. Add *one-fourth* of the flour mixture, beating on low speed just till moistened. Repeat beating in flour mixture by fourths.

Thoroughly wash beaters. In a large mixing bowl beat egg whites and cream of tartar on medium to high speed till soft peaks form (tips curl). Gradually add ½ cup sugar, *2 tablespoons* at a time, beating on medium to high speed till stiff peaks form (tips stand straight). Fold *1 cup* of the egg white mixture into egg yolk mixture. Then fold yolk mixture back into remaining egg white mixture. Pour batter into 2 greased and floured 8-inch round baking pans. Bake in a 325° oven for 30 to 35 minutes or till top springs back when lightly touched. Cool in pans on wire racks 5 minutes. Remove from pans; cool completely on wire racks. Split each cake layer horizontally into 2 layers.

In a chilled mixing bowl beat whipping cream, 3 tablespoons sugar, and vanilla till stiff peaks form. Place one cake layer on a cake plate. Spread with *one-fourth* of the whipped cream. Top with *one-fourth* of the berries. Repeat layers three times, ending with berries. Drizzle with melted white baking bar. Chill. Garnish with additional berries and White Filigree Leaves, if desired. Serves 12.

Nutrition facts per serving: 289 calories, 14 g total fat (8 g saturated fat), 112 mg cholesterol, 111 mg sodium, 36 g carbohydrate, 1 g fiber, 4 g protein.
Daily Value: 24% vitamin A, 14% vitamin C, 6% calcium, 6% iron.

CHOCOLATE-STRAWBERRY SHORTCAKES

Chocolate biscuits update this version of an American classic.

4 cups sliced strawberries
¼ cup sugar
1⅔ cups all-purpose flour
⅓ cup unsweetened cocoa powder
¼ cup sugar
1 tablespoon baking powder
¼ teaspoon salt
½ cup butter or margarine
1 beaten egg
⅔ cup milk
   Sweetened Whipped Cream
   Chocolate ice-cream topping
      (optional)
   Whole strawberries (optional)

Lightly grease a baking sheet. Combine sliced strawberries and the ¼ cup sugar. Set aside.

For shortcakes, in a medium mixing bowl combine flour, cocoa powder, the ¼ cup sugar, baking powder, and salt. Cut in butter or margarine till mixture resembles coarse crumbs. Combine egg and milk; add all at once to flour mixture and stir just till moistened. Drop dough into 6 portions on prepared baking sheet.

Bake in a 450° oven for 10 to 12 minutes or till a toothpick inserted in centers comes out clean. Cool slightly on a wire rack.

To serve, split warm shortcakes in half crosswise. Spoon a little Sweetened Whipped Cream on shortcake bottoms. Top with sliced strawberries. Add shortcake tops and top with remaining whipped cream. Drizzle with chocolate ice-cream topping and garnish with whole strawberries, if desired. Makes 6 servings.

Sweetened Whipped Cream: In a chilled small mixing bowl beat 1 cup *whipping cream*, 2 tablespoons *sugar,* and 1 teaspoon *vanilla* with an electric mixer on medium speed till soft peaks form.

Nutrition facts per serving: 546 calories, 33 g total fat (19 g saturated fat), 133 mg cholesterol, 466 mg sodium, 58 g carbohydrate, 3 g fiber, 8 g protein.
Daily Value: 35% vitamin A, 94% vitamin C, 25% calcium, 19% iron.

CHOOSE-A-FRUIT BAR COOKIES

Keep these yummy fruit-filled bars on hand in your freezer, and you'll have a delicious snack ready for kids, grown-ups, or drop-in guests.

2 cups peeled and finely chopped fresh or frozen fruit (peaches, nectarines, pears, apples, apricots, or bananas)
2 cups all-purpose flour
½ cup whole wheat flour
1 teaspoon apple pie spice or ground cinnamon
½ teaspoon baking powder
½ teaspoon baking soda
¼ teaspoon salt
⅔ cup sugar
½ cup butter or margarine
2 eggs
1 teaspoon vanilla
1 cup fruit juice or nectar (orange, apple, apricot, peach, or pear)
¾ cup chopped pecans (optional)
   Creamy Frosting
   Fresh fruit (optional)

Thaw and drain fruit, if frozen. Grease and lightly flour a 15x10x1-inch baking pan. In a medium mixing bowl stir together all-purpose flour, whole wheat flour, apple pie spice or cinnamon, baking powder, baking soda, and salt. Set aside.

In a large mixing bowl beat sugar and butter or margarine with an electric mixer on medium speed till fluffy. Add eggs and vanilla; beat well. Add flour mixture and desired fruit juice alternately to egg mixture, beating on low speed after each addition. Stir in chopped fruit, and, if desired, chopped nuts. Spread batter into prepared pan.

Bake in a 350° oven for 25 to 30 minutes or till a wooden toothpick inserted near the center comes out clean. Cool in pan on a wire rack. Spread Creamy Frosting over cooled bars. Cut into bars. Garnish with additional fresh fruit just before serving, if desired. Makes 24.

Creamy Frosting: In a mixing bowl beat ½ cup softened *butter or margarine* with an electric mixer on medium speed for 30 seconds. Gradually add 2 cups sifted *powdered sugar,* beating well. Beat in ¼ cup *fruit juice or nectar* (orange, apple, apricot, peach, or pear). Gradually beat in another 2 cups sifted *powdered sugar,* adding additional fruit juice, if necessary to make frosting a spreading consistency.

*Note: To freeze, allow frosting to dry. Wrap cut bars individually in plastic wrap and place in a covered, vapor-proof container. Thaw at room temperature for 30 minutes before serving.

Nutrition facts per serving: 215 calories, 8 g total fat (5 g saturated fat), 38 mg cholesterol, 139 mg sodium, 35 g carbohydrate, 1 g fiber, 2 g protein.
Daily Value: 8% vitamin A, 12% vitamin C, 1% calcium, 4% iron.

APRICOT-FILLED JELLY ROLL

Slices of this tender spice cake swirled with tangy sweet apricots make delectable treats for a bridal or baby shower or an afternoon tea.

½ cup all-purpose flour
1 teaspoon baking powder
1 teaspoon ground cinnamon
¼ teaspoon ground nutmeg
¼ teaspoon ground cloves
¼ teaspoon ground ginger
4 egg yolks
⅓ cup granulated sugar
4 egg whites
½ cup granulated sugar
   Sifted powdered sugar
1 pound fresh apricots (8 to 12),
      chopped (2½ cups)
⅓ cup water
3 tablespoons granulated sugar
4 teaspoons cornstarch
   Cream Cheese Frosting

Grease and flour a 15x10x1-inch baking pan; set aside. Mix flour, baking powder, cinnamon, nutmeg, cloves, and ginger; set aside. Beat egg yolks with an electric mixer on high speed for 5 minutes or till thick. Gradually add ⅓ cup sugar, beating on high speed till sugar is almost dissolved. Wash beaters.

Beat egg whites on medium to high speed till soft peaks form (tips curl). Add ½ cup sugar, *2 tablespoons* at a time, beating on medium to high speed till stiff peaks form (tips stand straight). Fold *1 cup* of egg white mixture into yolk mixture. Fold yolk mixture into remaining egg white mixture. Fold in flour mixture. Spread in prepared pan.

Bake in a 375° oven for 12 to 15 minutes or till cake springs back when touched. Immediately loosen cake from pan. Invert onto a towel sprinkled with powdered sugar. Roll up cake and towel, jelly-roll style, starting from one of the short sides. Cool.

Meanwhile, for filling, bring apricots and water to boiling; reduce heat. Cover; simmer for 5 minutes. Mix 3 tablespoons sugar and cornstarch. Stir into apricot mixture. Cook and stir till thickened and bubbly. Cook and stir 2 minutes more. Cool. *Do not stir.*

Unroll cake. Spread filling over cake. Roll up cake as before. Frost with Cream Cheese Frosting. Store in refrigerator. Serves 10.

Cream Cheese Frosting: Beat together one 3-ounce package *cream cheese;* ¼ cup *butter or margarine,* softened; and 1 teaspoon *vanilla.* Add 2 cups sifted *powdered sugar.* Beat till of spreading consistency.

Nutrition facts per serving: 308 calories, 10 g total fat (5 g saturated fat), 107 mg cholesterol, 135 mg sodium, 52 g carbohydrate, 1 g fiber, 4 g protein.
Daily Value: 32% vitamin A, 7% vitamin C, 5% calcium, 7% iron.

LEMON-POPPY SEED SHORTCAKE

Mascarpone, a soft Italian cheese, and whipping cream make an ultra-rich shortcake filling. Look for mascarpone cheese in large supermarkets, cheese shops, or Italian specialty stores.

6	cups cut up, peeled kiwi fruit, mangoes, or peaches; sliced strawberries; or whole raspberries or blueberries
¼	cup granulated sugar (optional)
2	cups all-purpose flour
1	tablespoon baking powder
½	teaspoon cream of tartar
¼	teaspoon baking soda
½	cup butter or margarine
¾	cup buttermilk or sour milk
2	tablespoons poppy seed
1	teaspoon finely shredded lemon peel
⅔	cup whipping cream
8	ounces mascarpone cheese or soft-style cream cheese
¾	cup sifted powdered sugar
½	teaspoon finely shredded lemon peel

In a medium mixing bowl stir together fresh fruit and, if desired, the ¼ cup granulated sugar. Set aside.

For the shortcake, in a medium mixing bowl combine the flour, baking powder, cream of tartar, and baking soda. Cut in the butter or margarine till mixture resembles coarse crumbs. Make a well in the center; add the buttermilk or sour milk, poppy seed, and the 1 teaspoon lemon peel all at once. Stir just till dough clings together.

On a lightly floured surface, knead dough gently for 10 to 12 strokes. Pat dough into an 8-inch circle on a baking sheet. Using a sharp knife, cut into 10 wedges, but *do not separate.* Bake in a 450° oven for 15 to 18 minutes or till golden.

Meanwhile, in a medium mixing bowl beat the whipping cream with an electric mixer on low speed just till soft peaks form. Add the mascarpone cheese or soft-style cream cheese, the ¾ cup powdered sugar, and the ½ teaspoon lemon peel. Beat till fluffy (the mixture will thicken as it is beaten).

Separate the warm shortcake into wedges. Split wedges. Pipe or spread the mascarpone cheese mixture over the bottom layers of the wedges. Spoon the fresh fruit onto the cheese layer. Add shortcake tops. Serve immediately. Pass any remaining fresh fruit. Serves 10.

Nutrition facts per serving: 404 calories, 27 g total fat (16 g saturated fat), 76 mg cholesterol, 274 mg sodium, 39 g carbohydrate, 2 g fiber, 9 g protein.
Daily Value: 32% vitamin A, 57% vitamin C, 14% calcium, 10% iron.

ORANGE-MACADAMIA NUT COOKIES

Bite into one of these melt-in-your-mouth morsels and savor the zingy orange flavor in both the buttery cookie and the creamy frosting.

4 cups all-purpose flour
2 cups sifted powdered sugar
1 cup cornstarch
2 cups butter (no substitutes)
1 cup chopped macadamia nuts or toasted walnuts
2 egg yolks, slightly beaten
1 tablespoon finely shredded orange peel
4 to 6 tablespoons orange juice
Granulated sugar
Orange Frosting
Finely shredded orange peel (optional)

In an extra large mixing bowl stir together flour, powdered sugar, and cornstarch. Using a pastry blender, cut in butter till mixture resembles coarse crumbs. Stir in nuts. Combine egg yolks, 1 tablespoon orange peel, and 4 tablespoons of the juice; add to flour mixture, stirring till moistened. If necessary, add remaining juice to moisten.

On a lightly floured surface, knead dough till it forms a ball. Shape dough into 1¼-inch balls. Arrange balls on an ungreased baking sheet. Flatten balls by pressing with the bottom of a glass to ¼-inch thickness, dipping glass into granulated sugar for each round.

Bake in a 350° oven for 12 to 15 minutes or till edges begin to brown. Remove from baking sheet. Cool on a wire rack. Frost with Orange Frosting. If desired, sprinkle with finely shredded orange peel. Makes 6 dozen.

Orange Frosting: In a mixing bowl stir together 2 cups sifted *powdered sugar*, 3 tablespoons softened *butter*, 1 teaspoon finely shredded *orange peel*, and enough *orange juice* (2 to 3 tablespoons) to make frosting of spreading consistency.

Nutrition facts per serving: 116 calories, 7 g total fat (4 g saturated fat), 21 mg cholesterol, 57 mg sodium, 13 g carbohydrate, 0 g fiber, 1 g protein.
Daily Value: 6% vitamin A, 1% vitamin C, 0% calcium, 2% iron.

APPLE CAKE WITH CARAMEL-RAISIN SAUCE

Brighten a cold, gray winter day with a wedge of this moist spice cake generously drizzled with warm caramel sauce.

2   cups all-purpose flour
¾   cup granulated sugar
½   cup packed brown sugar
2   teaspoons baking powder
1   teaspoon ground cinnamon
½   teaspoon baking soda
½   teaspoon salt
½   teaspoon ground ginger
¼   teaspoon ground cloves
2   eggs, slightly beaten
1   8-ounce carton dairy sour cream
¼   cup butter or margarine, melted
3   tablespoons milk
1   teaspoon vanilla
1   medium apple, peeled and coarsely
      shredded (1 cup)
⅔   cup chopped walnuts
      Caramel-Raisin Sauce

Grease and lightly flour an 8-inch springform pan or a 9x9x2-inch baking pan; set aside.

In a large mixing bowl stir together the 2 cups flour, granulated sugar, brown sugar, baking powder, cinnamon, baking soda, salt, ginger, and cloves. Make a well in the center of the flour mixture.

In a medium mixing bowl combine eggs, sour cream, melted butter or margarine, milk, and vanilla. Add egg mixture all at once to dry ingredients. Stir just till moistened. Fold in shredded apple and nuts. Spread batter in the prepared pan.

Bake in a 350° oven about 50 minutes for springform pan or about 45 minutes for 9x9x2-inch pan, or till a wooden toothpick inserted near the center comes out clean. Cool in pan on a wire rack for 20 minutes. Remove sides of the springform pan. Serve warm or cool with Caramel-Raisin Sauce. Makes 12 servings.

Caramel-Raisin Sauce: In a medium saucepan melt ½ cup *butter or margarine.* Stir in 1 cup packed *brown sugar* and 2 tablespoons *light corn syrup.* Cook and stir over medium heat until mixture comes to a full boil. Stir in ½ cup *whipping cream.* Return to a full boil. Remove from heat. Stir in ¼ cup *raisins.* Serve warm.

Nutrition facts per serving: 460 calories, 24 g total fat (13 g saturated fat), 88 mg cholesterol, 355 mg sodium, 58 g carbohydrate, 1 g fiber, 5 g protein.
Daily Value: 21% vitamin A, 1% vitamin C, 11% calcium, 14% iron.

DOUBLE RASPBERRY CHEESECAKE

Indulge in a slice of this raspberry-studded, ricotta cheesecake topped with a glistening red raspberry sauce.

1½ cups finely crushed graham crackers
¼   cup butter or margarine, melted
2   8-ounce packages cream cheese, softened
1   cup ricotta cheese
1¼ cups sugar
3   tablespoons all-purpose flour
1   teaspoon lemon extract
3   eggs, slightly beaten
⅔   cup red raspberries
    Raspberry Sauce

For crust, in a small mixing bowl combine crushed graham crackers and melted butter or margarine. Press crumb mixture firmly onto the bottom and about 1½ inches up the sides of a 9-inch springform pan. Set aside.

In large mixing bowl combine cream cheese, ricotta cheese, sugar, flour, and lemon extract. Beat with an electric mixer on low speed till combined. Add eggs all at once and beat on low speed just till combined. Gently fold in raspberries. Pour into prepared pan.

Bake in a 375° oven for 35 to 40 minutes or till center appears nearly set when shaken. Cool for 15 minutes. Loosen crust from sides of pan. Cool 30 minutes more; remove sides of pan. Cover and chill for 4 to 24 hours. Serve with Raspberry Sauce. Makes 12 servings.

Raspberry Sauce: In a medium saucepan stir together 1 cup *raspberry-cranberry juice cocktail* and 1 tablespoon *cornstarch*. Cook and stir till thickened and bubbly. Add ¼ cup *currant jelly*, stirring until melted. Remove from heat. Stir in 1 cup *fresh or thawed, frozen red raspberries* and, if desired, 1 tablespoon *crème de cassis*. Cover and chill till serving time.

Nutrition facts per serving: 390 calories, 21 g total fat (12 g saturated fat), 112 mg cholesterol, 254 mg sodium, 43 g carbohydrate., 1 g fiber, 8g protein.
Daily Value: 25% vitamin A, 18% vitamin C, 8% calcium, 9% iron

STRAWBERRY-CHOCOLATE-PECAN TORTE

What could be simpler? You mix the batter for this spectacular torte in your electric blender.

2   tablespoons all-purpose flour
1   teaspoon baking powder
1   teaspoon finely shredded orange peel
4   eggs
¾   cup sugar
2½   cups pecans
1   cup miniature semisweet
      chocolate pieces
    Whipped Cream Frosting
1½   cups sliced strawberries
    Whole strawberries (optional)

Grease and lightly flour two 8x1½-inch round baking pans. Stir together flour, baking powder, and orange peel. Set pans and flour mixture aside.

In a blender container place eggs and sugar. Cover and blend till mixed. Add pecans. Blend about 1 minute more or till nearly smooth, stopping and scraping down sides as necessary. Transfer mixture to a mixing bowl. Stir in flour mixture. Stir in chocolate pieces. Spread batter evenly in prepared pans. Bake in a 350° oven for 20 to 25 minutes or till a toothpick inserted near the centers of the cakes comes out clean. Cool cakes in pans on wire racks for 10 minutes. Remove cakes from pans and cool completely on wire racks.

To assemble, place 1 cake layer on a platter. Pipe or spread with *1 cup* of the Whipped Cream Frosting. Arrange sliced strawberries over frosting, overlapping slightly. Decorate with whole strawberries, if desired. Makes 12 servings.

Whipped Cream Frosting: In a 1-cup glass measuring cup combine 2 tablespoons *cold water* and 1 teaspoon *unflavored gelatin.* Let stand for 2 minutes. Fill a saucepan with about 2 inches water; bring to boiling. Place measuring cup containing gelatin mixture in the boiling water. Heat and stir about 1 minute or till gelatin is completely dissolved. Remove from heat. Cool slightly. In a medium mixing bowl beat 1½ cups *whipping cream,* 3 tablespoons *sugar,* and ½ teaspoon finely shredded *orange peel* with an electric mixer on medium speed while gradually drizzling the gelatin mixture over the cream mixture. Continue beating just till stiff peaks form. Use immediately.

Nutrition facts per serving: 415 calories, 32 g total fat (9 g saturated fat), 112 mg cholesterol, 64 mg sodium, 32 g carbohydrate, 2 g fiber, 6 g protein.
***Daily Value:** 16% vitamin A, 19% vitamin C, 5% calcium, 8% iron.*

CHERRY-CREAM CHEESE ROLL

For another time, ladle the almond-scented cherry sauce over scoops of vanilla or chocolate ice cream.

½   cup all-purpose flour
½   teaspoon baking powder
½   teaspoon ground cinnamon
½   teaspoon ground cloves
¼   teaspoon ground nutmeg
¼   teaspoon salt
4   egg yolks
1   teaspoon vanilla
¼   cup granulated sugar
¼   cup packed brown sugar
4   egg whites
¼   cup granulated sugar
    Sifted powdered sugar
    Cream Cheese-Cherry Filling
    Cherry Sauce

Grease and flour a 15x10x1-inch baking pan. In a bowl combine flour, baking powder, cinnamon, cloves, nutmeg, and salt. Set aside. Beat egg yolks and vanilla with electric mixer on high speed 5 minutes or till thick. Gradually add the ¼ cup sugar and brown sugar, beating on high speed till sugar is nearly dissolved. Wash beaters.

Beat egg whites on medium to high speed till soft peaks form (tips curl). Gradually add the ¼ cup sugar beating till stiff peaks form (tips stand straight). Fold yolk mixture into beaten whites. Sprinkle flour mixture over egg mixture; fold in till mixed. Spread in prepared pan.

Bake in 375° oven for 12 to 15 minutes or till cake springs back when touched lightly. Immediately loosen edges from pan and turn out onto towel sprinkled with powdered sugar. Roll up towel and cake, starting from one of the short sides. Cool on a wire rack.

Unroll cake; remove towel. Spread cake with Cream Cheese-Cherry Filling. Roll up cake. Store in the refrigerator up to 24 hours. Serve with warm Cherry Sauce. Makes 10 servings.

Cream Cheese-Cherry Filling: Beat one 8-ounce package *cream cheese,* softened; ¼ cup *butter or margarine,* softened; and 1 teaspoon *vanilla* with an electric mixer till combined. Beat in 1 cup sifted *powdered sugar.* Stir in ¼ cup chopped, pitted *dark sweet cherries.*

Cherry Sauce: In a saucepan mix ¼ cup *granulated sugar* and 1 tablespoon *cornstarch.* Add ½ cup *apple juice* and 2 cups pitted *dark sweet cherries.* Cook and stir till bubbly. Cook and stir two minutes more. Remove from heat. Stir in ½ teaspoon *almond extract.* Serve warm.

Nutrition facts per serving: 319 calories, 15 g total fat (9 g saturated fat), 123 mg cholesterol, 213 mg sodium, 42 g carbohydrate., 1 g fiber, 5 g protein
Daily Value: 27% vitamin A, 3% vitamin C, 4% calcium, 7% iron

CRANBERRY PINWHEELS

Orange marmalade and cranberries team up for a sweet-tart filling in these delightful cookies.

1   cup cranberries
¼   cup orange marmalade
1   tablespoon honey
⅔   cup butter or margarine
½   cup granulated sugar
1   teaspoon baking powder
½   teaspoon finely shredded orange peel
1   egg
1   tablespoon milk
1   teaspoon vanilla
2   cups all-purpose flour
    Powdered Sugar Frosting
¼   cup finely chopped walnuts

For filling, cook cranberries, marmalade, and honey in a covered saucepan over low heat till mixture boils and berries pop. Uncover and cook, stirring occasionally, about 8 minutes more or till mixture is the consistency of thick jam. Cool.

Beat the butter or margarine with an electric mixer on medium to high speed for 30 seconds. Add the sugar, baking powder, and orange peel and beat till combined. Beat in egg, milk, and vanilla till combined. Beat in as much of the flour as you can with the mixer. Stir in any remaining flour with a wooden spoon. Divide dough in half. Cover; chill about 3 hours or till easy to handle.

On a lightly floured surface roll each half of dough into a 10-inch square. Cut each half into sixteen 2½-inch squares. Place squares 2 inches apart on an ungreased cookie sheet.

Cut 1-inch slits from each corner to the center of each square. Spoon ¾ teaspoon of the filling on the center of each square. Fold every other point to the center to form a pinwheel. Pinch points together to seal. (If necessary to seal, lightly moisten points with water.)

Bake in a 375° oven for 8 to 10 minutes or till points just begin to turn brown. Remove and cool on a wire rack. Drizzle with Powdered Sugar Frosting. Sprinkle nuts in center of cookies. Makes 32.

Powdered Sugar Frosting: Combine ½ cup sifted *powdered sugar* and a few drops *vanilla*. Stir in 2 teaspoons *milk*. Add additional milk, a small amount at a time, to make an icing of drizzling consistency.

Nutrition facts per serving: 97 calories, 5 g total fat (2 g saturated fat), 17 mg cholesterol, 53 mg sodium, 13 g carbohydrate, 1 g fiber, 1 g protein.
Daily Value: 3% vitamin A, 1% vitamin C, 1% calcium, 2% iron.

CHOCOLATE CHIP-BANANA CAKE

Keep this easy-to-tote snack cake in mind for picnics, potlucks, or whenever it's your turn to bring treats.

1¾ cups all-purpose flour
 1 cup granulated sugar
 ½ cup packed brown sugar
1½ teaspoons baking powder
 ½ teaspoon baking soda
 1 cup mashed ripe banana (3 medium)
 ½ cup dairy sour cream
 ½ cup butter or margarine, softened
 1 teaspoon vanilla
 2 eggs
 1 cup miniature semisweet
   chocolate pieces
   Sifted powdered sugar

Grease a 13x9x2-inch baking pan; set aside.

In a large mixing bowl stir together flour, granulated sugar, brown sugar, baking powder, and baking soda. Add mashed banana, sour cream, softened butter or margarine, and vanilla. Beat with an electric mixer on low to medium speed till combined. Then beat on medium speed for 1 minute, scraping sides of bowl occasionally. Add eggs and beat 1 minute more. Stir in chocolate pieces. Pour batter into the prepared pan, spreading evenly.

Bake in a 350° oven for 35 to 40 minutes or till a wooden toothpick inserted near the center comes out clean. Cool completely in pan on a wire rack. Sprinkle with sifted powdered sugar. Serves 24.

Nutrition facts per serving: 170 calories, 7 g total fat (3 g saturated fat), 30 mg cholesterol, 100 mg sodium, 27 g carbohydrate, 0 g fiber, 2 g protein.
Daily Value: 5% vitamin A, 1% vitamin C, 3% calcium, 5% iron.

BAVARIAN APPLE CHEESECAKE

For a change of pace, try this apple-topped cheesecake for a Thanksgiving or Christmas dessert.

⅓ cup sugar
⅓ cup butter or margarine
1 tablespoon shortening
¼ teaspoon vanilla
1 cup all-purpose flour
⅛ teaspoon salt
4 cups peeled, cored, and sliced apples
2 8-ounce packages cream cheese
½ cup granulated sugar
½ teaspoon vanilla
2 eggs
⅓ cup sugar
1 teaspoon ground cinnamon
¼ cup sliced almonds

In a medium mixing bowl beat the ⅓ cup sugar, butter or margarine, shortening, and the ¼ teaspoon vanilla on medium speed of an electric mixer till combined. Stir in flour and salt till crumbly. Pat into the bottom of a 9-inch springform pan. Set aside.

Place apple slices in a single layer in a shallow baking pan. Cover with foil. Bake in a 400° oven for 15 minutes.

Meanwhile, for filling, in a large mixing bowl beat the cream cheese, the ½ cup sugar, and the ½ teaspoon vanilla with an electric mixer on medium to high speed till fluffy. Add the eggs all at once, beating on low speed just till combined. Pour into pastry-lined pan. Arrange warm apple slices over filling. Combine the remaining ⅓ cup sugar and cinnamon. Sprinkle filling with sugar mixture and almonds.

Bake in a 375° oven about 35 minutes or till center appears nearly set when shaken. Cool for 15 minutes. Loosen crust from sides of pan. Cool 30 minutes more; remove sides of pan. Cover and chill for 4 to 24 hours. Makes 12 servings.

Nutrition facts per serving: 245 calories, 22 g total fat (12 g saturated fat), 91 mg cholesterol, 198 mg sodium, 34 g carbohydrate, 1 g fiber, 6 g protein.
Daily Value: 22% vitamin A, 3% vitamin C, 4% calcium, 8% iron.

CRANBERRY POUND CAKE

Ruby red cranberries and a delicate orange flavor give this moist and tender cake a holiday flair.

1   cup butter (no substitutes)
6   eggs
½   cup dairy sour cream
3   cups all-purpose flour
1   teaspoon baking powder
¼   teaspoon baking soda
2   teaspoons finely shredded orange
    peel (set aside)
⅓   cup orange juice
2   cups sugar
1½   cups chopped cranberries
    Orange Icing

Let butter, eggs, and sour cream stand at room temperature for 30 minutes.

Grease and lightly flour a 10-inch fluted tube pan; set aside. Combine the 3 cups flour, baking powder, and baking soda; set aside. Combine sour cream and orange juice; set aside.

In a large mixer bowl beat butter with a freestanding electric mixer on medium speed about 30 seconds or till softened. Gradually add sugar, about *2 tablespoons* at a time, beating on medium speed about 8 minutes total or till very light and fluffy. Add eggs, one at a time, beating on medium speed for 1 minute after adding each egg, and scraping the bowl often. Add flour alternately with sour cream mixture, beating at low speed just till combined. Fold in cranberries and orange peel.

Pour batter into prepared pan. Bake in a 325° oven for 1 hour 15 minutes to 1 hour 20 minutes or till a wooden toothpick inserted near the center comes out clean. Cool cake in pan on a wire rack for 10 minutes. Remove cake from pan and cool completely. Drizzle Orange Icing over cake. Makes 16 to 20 servings.

Orange Icing: In a small mixing bowl combine 1½ cups sifted *powdered sugar* and ½ teaspoon finely shredded *orange peel.* Stir in 1 to 2 tablespoons *orange juice* to make icing of drizzling consistency.

Nutrition facts per serving: 363 calories, 15 g total fat (9 g saturated fat), 114 mg cholesterol, 187 mg sodium, 53 g carbohydrate., 1 g fiber, 5 g protein.
Daily Value: 15% vitamin A, 8% vitamin C, 3% calcium, 9% iron.

Keep track of your daily nutrition needs by using the information we provide at the end of each recipe. We've analyzed the nutritional content of each recipe serving for you. When a recipe gives an ingredient substitution, we used the first choice in the analysis. If it makes a range of servings (such as 4 to 6), we used the smallest number. Ingredients listed as optional weren't included in the calculations.

METRIC COOKING HINTS

By making a few conversions, cooks in Australia, Canada, and the United Kingdom can use the recipes in Better Homes and Gardens® *Fruit Desserts* with confidence. The charts on this page provide a guide for converting measurements from the U.S. customary system, which is used throughout this book, to the imperial and metric systems. There also is a conversion table for oven temperatures to accommodate the differences in oven calibrations.

Volume and Weight: Americans traditionally use cup measures for liquid and solid ingredients. The chart (top right) shows the approximate imperial and metric equivalents. If you are accustomed to weighing solid ingredients, here are some helpful approximate equivalents.
■ 1 cup butter, caster sugar, or rice = 8 ounces = about 250 grams
■ 1 cup flour = 4 ounces = about 125 grams
■ 1 cup icing sugar = 5 ounces = about 150 grams
   Spoon measures are used for smaller amounts of ingredients. Although the size of the tablespoon varies slightly among countries, for practical purposes and for recipes in this book, a straight substitution is all that's necessary.
   Measurements made using cups or spoons should always be level, unless stated otherwise.

Product Differences: Most of the ingredients called for in the recipes in this book are available in English-speaking countries. However, some are known by different names. Here are some common American ingredients and their possible counterparts:
■ Sugar is granulated or caster sugar.
■ Powdered sugar is icing sugar.
■ All-purpose flour is plain household flour or white flour. When self-rising flour is used in place of all-purpose flour in a recipe that calls for leavening, omit the leavening agent (baking soda or baking powder) and salt.
■ Light corn syrup is golden syrup.
■ Cornstarch is cornflour.
■ Baking soda is bicarbonate of soda.
■ Vanilla is vanilla essence.
■ Green, red, or yellow sweet peppers are capsicums.
■ Sultanas are golden raisins.

USEFUL EQUIVALENTS: U.S = AUST./BR.

⅛ teaspoon = 0.5 ml
¼ teaspoon = 1 ml
½ teaspoon = 2 ml
1 teaspoon = 5 ml
1 tablespoon = 1 tablespoon
¼ cup = 2 tablespoons = 2 fluid ounces = 60 ml
⅓ cup = ¼ cup = 3 fluid ounces = 90 ml
½ cup = ⅓ cup = 4 fluid ounces = 120 ml

⅔ cup = ½ cup = 5 fluid ounces = 150 ml
¾ cup = ⅔ cup = 6 fluid ounces = 180 ml
1 cup = ¾ cup = 8 fluid ounces = 240 ml
1¼ cups = 1 cup
2 cups = 1 pint
1 quart = 1 litre
½ inch = 1.27 centimetres
1 inch = 2.54 centimetres

BAKING PAN SIZES

American	Metric
8x1½-inch round baking pan	20x4-centimetre cake tin
9x1½-inch round baking pan	23x3.5-centimetre cake tin
11x7x1½-inch baking pan	28x18x4-centimetre baking tin
13x9x2-inch baking pan	30x20x3-centimetre baking tin
2-quart rectangular baking dish	30x20x3-centimetre baking tin
15x10x2-inch baking pan	30x25x2-centimetre baking tin (Swiss roll tin)
9-inch pie plate	22x4- or 23x4-centimetre pie plate
7- or 8-inch springform pan	18- or 20-centimetre springform or loose-bottom cake tin
9x5x3-inch loaf pan	23x13x7-centimetre or 2-pound narrow loaf tin or paté tin
1½-quart casserole	1.5-litre casserole
2-quart casserole	2-litre casserole

OVEN TEMPERATURE EQUIVALENTS

Fahrenheit Setting	Celsius Setting*	Gas Setting
300°F	150°C	Gas Mark 2 (slow)
325°F	160°C	Gas Mark 3 (moderately slow)
350°F	180°C	Gas Mark 4 (moderate)
375°F	190°C	Gas Mark 5 (modcratcly hot)
400°F	200°C	Gas Mark 6 (hot)
425°F	220°C	Gas Mark 7
450°F	230°C	Gas Mark 8 (very hot)
Broil		Grill

*Electric and gas ovens may be calibrated using Celsius. However, increase the Celsius setting 10 to 20 degrees when cooking above 160°C with an electric oven. For convection or forced-air ovens (gas or electric), lower the temperature setting 10°C when cooking at all heat levels.